"Lynne's thoughtful, humble [...] tool for women today. We a[...] insecurities in this world where false images of per[...] media. *Sacred Refuge* candidly points us to the only truly safe space, the overwhelming love and tender care of culture-defying Jesus. It's a journey none of us can make alone, so Lynne's focus on community, or sacred sisterhood, is particularly important."

—Ellen Vaughn, *New York Times* best-selling author of *Being Elisabeth Elliot* and coauthor of *Jesus Revolution*

"Women need more than a safe place to shelter. They need sacred sisters to walk arm in arm with through storms and sunshine. *Sacred Refuge* provides stories that resonate with us and connect us with other women at the heart level. The beauty of this book is that it's saturated with God's truth and delivered in such a way that we want to discuss what we read with others. Read this book to discover God's love at a sacred level."

—Linda Goldfarb, international speaker, author, and board-certified Christian life coach

"Reading *Sacred Refuge* feels like gathering around the campfire on a summer beach, listening to friends share stories of God's sheltering them in difficult times. With compassion and creativity, Lynne Rienstra opens up the Scriptures and her life to offer comfort, strength, and hope to women facing life's challenges. If you long to find safety in the storm, this book is for you."

—Gwenfair Walters Adams, professor and director of spiritual formation studies at Gordon-Conwell Theological Seminary

"We all long to find refuge, that safe space where we feel seen, known, protected, and provided for. In Lynne Rienstra's *Sacred Refuge*, there is help, hope, and healing and, best of all, a solid, secure, and sacred connection with our loving, kind, peace-filled Creator, who breathes life into us and gives us a future to look forward to living."

—Pam Farrel, best-selling author of *Men Are Like Waffles, Women Are Like Spaghetti* and *Glimpse of God's Glory*

"Only a sister who has known deep loss can write of the profound love of her heavenly Father with equal depth. Only a writer sensitive to both spiritual style and substance can wrap fresh words around ancient biblical stories to speak incisively to women today. Only an apt student of Scripture can convey timeless truth that is biblically rooted and theologically sound. In *Sacred Refuge*'s author Lynne Rienstra, we have all this and much more. With winsome transparency, Rienstra invites women to move out of suffering and brokenness and into a sacred sisterhood as God's beautiful, beloved daughters."

—Maggie Wallem Rowe, speaker and author of *This Life We Share*

"Trade your performing, pleasing, and proving for the sacred refuge found in God. Author Lynne Rienstra has provided a path for when crisis crashes in, fear overwhelms, and you feel alone—a path for you to secure rest in the One who pursues, protects, and promises a future."

—PeggySue Wells, best-selling author of *Rediscovering Your Happily Ever After* and *The 10 Best Decisions a Single Mom Can Make*

"*Sacred Refuge* speaks to the deepest longings of the human heart: to be fully known and eternally secure. This book is ideal for small group engagement as it challenges us to run toward our Father and rest in his love in the context of community."

—Karen Hodge, coordinator of women's ministry for the Presbyterian Church in America and coauthor of *Life-giving Leadership*

"I've been blessed to know Lynne Rienstra for more than forty years. She is, without question, the most winsome woman of God I've ever met. Her love for Jesus is contagious, and her genuine affection for people shines throughout this book. I pray many women will find rest for their souls in the pages of *Sacred Refuge*."

—Donna Partow, author of *Becoming the Woman God Wants Me to Be*

Sacred Refuge

FINDING UNEXPECTED SHELTER IN YOUR CRISIS

Lynne Rienstra

KREGEL
PUBLICATIONS

Sacred Refuge: Finding Unexpected Shelter in Your Crisis
© 2024 by E. Lynne Rienstra

Published by Kregel Publications, a division of Kregel Inc., 2450 Oak Industrial Dr. NE, Grand Rapids, MI 49505. www.kregel.com.

Published in association with the Books & Such Literary Management, www.booksandsuch.com.

The persons and events portrayed in this book have been used with permission. To protect the privacy of these individuals, some names and identifying details have been changed.

Cataloging-in-Publication Data is available from the Library of Congress.

ISBN 978-0-8254-4871-3, print
ISBN 978-0-8254-7439-2, epub
ISBN 978-0-8254-7438-5, Kindle

Printed in the United States of America
24 25 26 27 28 29 30 31 32 33 / 5 4 3 2 1

For Rob, who has sheltered me these many years and loved me as Jesus loves the church.

He who dwells in the shelter of the Most High
will abide in the shadow of the Almighty.
I will say to the Lord, *"My refuge and my fortress,*
my God, in whom I trust."

For he will deliver you from the snare of the fowler
and from the deadly pestilence.
He will cover you with his pinions,
and under his wings you will find refuge.

*—*Psalm 91:1–4

Contents

From the Author's Heart

WHEN CRISIS FIRST careened into my life at age four—as my father left our family—I felt like I had just swallowed a pill and burst, gasping for breath, into the dystopia of the matrix. Only it was all too real.

Many years later, when I first witnessed sacred refuge, it felt like waking from a distant nightmare into the fulfillment of my heart's deepest desires.

I was well into my thirties, living in New England, and God had provided many opportunities for me to speak to women. A query from an inner-city church in Boston was one of them: "We are looking for a one-day retreat on the topic 'The Bride of Christ.'"

"I can do that," I replied.

Poring over Scripture, commentaries, and Strong's concordance, I was on the job. I pulled together two tidy, theologically sound talks on how the church is the Bride of Christ. There was only one problem: I lacked the heart of the message.

Four days from the event, I finally cried out to God with the question, "Father, what do you want me to tell these women?"

Moments later, I sensed the Holy Spirit urging me: *Tell them they are beautiful to me.*

Mic drop.

On the day of the retreat, I arrived at the church and was met by several security-detail men who escorted me safely past a crack house and garbage piled on the sidewalk. As I got settled and met some of the women, I remember thinking, *You're in over your head here, girl.*

This wasn't my regular gig, which typically included nicely dressed

suburban women with quiet voices welcoming me and introducing me
to various other nice women who thanked me politely for coming. This
was a free-for-all of raw, real life. It was wild. And it was wonderful.

After my first talk, we headed downstairs from the sanctuary for
lunch. Then it all broke open. One woman after another approached
me, often grabbing my elbow and forcibly leading me into a corner to
ask me, "Can I tell you what Jesus has done for me?"

Uhhhh, yes.

Out of their mouths tumbled one story after another of hardship,
struggle, and pain. These sisters were duking it out in a war zone.
Husbands gone MIA. Children taken as prisoners of war, captured by
gangs and hooked on heroin. Cancer diagnoses with no health insurance. Being dumped on the streets with their kids in the middle of
winter because they couldn't pay their rent.

Their daily fight for survival included no safety nets. I listened, rapt
and breathless. Standing there in my coordinated outfit and styled
hair, I knew I was in new territory.

When their hardscrabble stories were finished, each woman would
stop, look me in the eyes, and say, "But for Jesus. Oh, Lynne, let me tell
you what he has done for me. Jesus . . ." And they would be off, telling
tales of the specific ways Jesus had covered, cared for, or carried them
through their crises.

It was a wonder to witness, and I almost took my shoes off. Surely I
was on holy ground.

The women were beautiful. They glowed. Most wore no makeup.
Some of their smiles revealed missing teeth. Few had a moment to
comb their hair, much less money for a trip to a stylist. But to me, they
appeared like a radiant bride when she locks eyes with her bridegroom
on her way to the altar. Caught in lives where there was nothing and
no one else to protect them, they had thrown their whole hearts into a
fully dependent and fervent love affair with Jesus.

The women I taught in Boston that day became my professors. In
their pure passion for Jesus—in whom they had found real shelter in

their shelterless world—they showed me what *sacred refuge* looks like.

I drove back to Cape Cod that night, processing what I had experienced. On that dark road, suddenly and softly, I sensed the Holy Spirit's presence. *I dwell in the midst of brokenness.*

As that profound truth seeped into my spirit, the Lord gently invited me to stop trying so hard to look like I had it all together. I didn't. He knew that. I knew that. So why all the pretending? He invited me to start getting real with him and others. He invited me to stop trying to protect myself, to stop trying to be my own savior, and simply come to Jesus. He opened up the possibility that my problems (like those of my sisters in Boston) might be portals through which I could experience true protection in God's presence, as they had.

Witnessing these sisters' consuming love for Jesus as their *only* shelter turned out to be God's engraved invitation for me to follow the deepest longings of my heart—to be loved, seen, forgiven, provided for, comforted, and more—to the place where Jesus offered me all this in himself. It was a holy invitation out of hiding and into sacred refuge.

You likely face storms and struggles that make you long for refuge too. A badly broken relationship. Miscarriage or infertility. Caring for a spouse or parent with Alzheimer's. An unexpected diagnosis. A financial setback. Children or grandchildren who are walking away from God. A life-altering accident. Crises can leave us feeling overwhelmed, scared, and alone. Add to that the increasing complexity of everyday life, and our souls can feel battered from living on high alert.

Sister, if you've picked up this book, you long for a safe and peaceful place in the middle of it all. I know, because that's been my lifelong quest. God has lit up the path to shelter for me, and it's my heart's desire to help you find it for yourself. As you seek your own sacred refuge in the pages of this book, here is my prayer for you:

> *Father, you are our good and trustworthy Abba. Jesus, you are our loving and ever-present Bridegroom. Spirit, you are*

our Comforter and power source. Apart from you we can do nothing.

You know the woman holding this book. You designed and knit her together in her mother's womb. You know every purpose for which you created her and the good works you have prepared in advance for her to walk in. You know the problems that weigh her down, the crisis that has blown up in her life.

Oh wise and sovereign God, embedded in this crisis is your promise to bring good out of the worst of circumstances. I ask you not to waste anything in this hard season my sister walks through now. I ask you to bind the enemy's schemes against her and release—even through this crisis—every good gift and opportunity for growth attached to this trial. Lord, would you grant her the unexpected gift of shelter right in the middle of her storm?

Pour hope into her spirit as she reads. Let her hear your voice inviting her to make you her dwelling place and sacred refuge. May she find her place nestled under your wings (Psalm 91). Oh God, may this be your work, for your daughter, for your glory!

I ask this in the strong name of Jesus Christ. Amen.

Introduction

WHEN CRISIS KNOCKS us down so hard we cannot catch our breath, what our hearts most crave is refuge. Through my work with an international relief ministry, I have seen the effects of crisis around the globe: the look in a refugee girl's hollow eyes as she queues up for emergency feeding, the heart-wrenching brokenness in a grandmother who has lost a daughter and two grandsons to mortar fire, the shock etched on a pastor's wife's face two days after a hurricane decimated her town. Crisis carves us out and leaves us longing for shelter. Thankfully, such a place exists for those who know God.

Running from Saul, David called God his "refuge" and "strong tower" (Psalm 61:3). Martin Luther knew God as a "mighty fortress" (see Psalm 31:3). In the pit of a concentration camp, Corrie ten Boom found God to be her "hiding place" (Psalm 32:7). When her first husband, Jim, was martyred, Elisabeth Elliot experienced God's "everlasting arms" (Deuteronomy 33:27).

So for us, today, dealing with crises of our own, what is *sacred refuge*? And how can we experience it ourselves?

The word *sacred* refers to that which is "consecrated to or belonging to the divinity or a deity; holy."[1] It stands in contrast with what is secular, or of this world. If something is sacred, it is holy and never to be broken or dishonored. It is pure, protected, and unassailable.

Add to that the meaning of *refuge*: "shelter or protection from danger, difficulty, etc. . . . . a place of safety."[2] A refuge offers us asylum and safe harbor when life's storms hit.

Sacred refuge, then, is that place where God dwells with us, his people, and invites us to dwell deeply in him. It is promised in the covenant of grace God gave to the children of Israel: "I will walk among you and will be your God, and you shall be my people" (Leviticus 26:12). It is fulfilled in the bride's joyful cry regarding her Bridegroom in Song of Solomon: "My beloved is mine, and I am his" (2:16).

Sacred refuge is that place where God dwells with us, his people, and invites us to dwell deeply in him.

Sacred refuge is the meeting place of our brokenness and heaven's wholeness. It is made possible by Jesus Christ, God with us. He came to earth, put on flesh, and suffered with and among us. In living perfectly, dying in our place, giving us his righteousness, and rising from the dead, Jesus became the holy haven our shattered hearts long for. He is the cornerstone (Ephesians 2:20) and door (John 10:7) of the sacred refuge God invites us to enter. He is the light of the world in a world of darkness (John 8:12), the bread of life in a world of hunger (John 6:48), and the Good Shepherd in a world of wolves (John 10:11).

The Old Testament recounts the provision of "cities of refuge."[3] These were safe spaces where those who were guilty of an unintentional crime could live without recrimination. Similarly, in times past, church buildings were set apart as places of refuge for those running for their lives. But what if there is a place more indestructible than bricks and mortar edifices? More trustworthy than Old Faithful? More satisfying than the "other lovers" we have sought to save us?

Many of us have visited that safe place in God.

Perhaps it happened the night you almost lost a child in the ER. The moment you heard you had cancer. The day you discovered your marriage was over. Crises like these catapult us into God's waiting arms.

However, in time, life returns to normal and we politely tell God, "Thanks. I've got it from here."

I've been there and done that. But God invited me to make a significant shift as I wrote this book through a cancer diagnosis, a devastating car accident while on the way home from surgery to remove the cancer, and an unexpected course correction to this book. My crises, though uncomfortable, became the catalyst for my permanent change of address. I shifted from occasionally visiting God's shelter to making it—making him—my home. It was a move both scary and glorious. My hope is that you experience a similar "moving day" in these pages, a radical shift in your spiritual address.

By the way, it's the perfect time to relocate. Because the times, they are a-changin'.

Looking for a Hideout

For a while now, you may have woken in a state of panic. *What will today bring? What new problems will demand my attention? How will I be pulled in yet another direction?* We're living in volatile and uncertain times, with new crises and conflicts emerging daily that threaten to tear our culture and world apart.

Many of us are stumbling through our days, just trying to get through it all. Pay the next bill. Keep the kids rolling through school. Fight traffic. Fight with our husbands. Fight our belly fat. Fight the good fight.

Like me, you may look at the state of our world and fight the urge to cash in your 401(k) and move to an island. Tempting, but I'm pretty sure that's not God's plan for us at this moment.

The times we live in may feel scary, but God has so much better for us than hiding. He has so much more for us in his presence. In love and compassion, he's inviting us—right in the midst of our crises—to begin living under the shadow of his wings (see Psalm 91:4). Not just retreating there every once in a while or running to it when we hear the piercing sirens, but actually *dwelling* there every day.

So often, though, we hide from the stress and chaos of life in places outside of God's arms. Many of us are hiding out in our own lives, year after year. Some of us are hiding, as I have, in plain sight.

Suzanne hides in her faithful workout regimen. Hilary, in food. Kaneisha hides in perfectionism. Jen, in an R-rated Netflix series that seems to satisfy something missing in her life. Taylor, in steamy bodice-ripper novels. Chen hides in busyness. Maria, in becoming the world's best mom. Jill hides in her growing investment portfolio. Kaitlyn, in pursuit of the corner office. Tanya hides in her social media feeds.

Some of us are hiding in excuses that feel real but fall short of all God offers us in Jesus:

- "I tried Christianity, but I'm still broken and disappointed. Why try again?"
- "I'm caught in an endless cycle of sin. God has to be sick of my failure by now."
- "I've had too many losses. I'm not sure I can open myself to God anymore."
- "Life hasn't gone the way I thought it would. I don't think I can trust God."

The enemy of our souls loves all this. It was his idea from the start to send us hiding. He's downright terrified of what will happen when God's daughters shake off the spiritual slumber of their hiding places and start living from sacred refuge.

What might happen if we began powerfully fulfilling our God-given design as life-givers (both spiritual and physical)? What if, having been sheltered ourselves, we begin to shelter others? That would grow God's kingdom. That could change the world!

And the enemy can't have that.

Satan is threatened by what happens when we finally enter—and live from—sacred refuge, and here's why. Sacred refuge is

- where we encounter God;
- where God tells us who we are;
- the place of knowing and being known;
- the place of healing;
- the place of renewal, rest, and refreshment;
- where God empowers us to live out our callings;
- where we discern God's voice and battle strategy; and
- where we begin to shelter others.

Sacred refuge is where we receive God's love and love him in return. It is the place we discover our life-altering identity as "the beloved."

Finding Sacred Refuge in a Sacred Sisterhood

We women love to hang out and hear each other's stories, don't we? In the pages of *Sacred Refuge*, you'll meet ten modern women whose lives probably look a lot like your own. Like you, they have faced a crisis that threatened to undo them. Only it didn't. Because God helped them find a safe place in him that sheltered them through their storm. You'll also meet ten biblical women who discovered God's loving refuge in their own times of crisis.

My prayer is that you will recognize your own narrative in their stories. They and the other women whose experiences fill this book are our sisters across time and space. Together we form a sacred sisterhood of both suffering (because of sin) and solace (because of Jesus). As we invite him in, he will dwell richly and powerfully in our midst as the center of our security and source of our safety.

Think of *Sacred Refuge* as a meeting place with other women who, like you, are looking for a path to that safe place. Together we will move from *finding* sacred refuge, to *abiding* in God's refuge, to *sharing* his refuge with others. Each chapter begins with a guiding question related to that chapter's theme and includes stories from your sacred sisters, discussions about how their stories connect to your own, a Transforming Truth, and a final invitation to hear Jesus's voice offering you sacred refuge in himself.

You can also apply what God is revealing to you at the end of each chapter in a final section titled "REST Under His Wings." This section will help you **R**elease control; **E**xchange your fear for God's love; **S**ee yourself in Christ; and **T**rust Jesus's power to shelter you. You may want to journal your answers to those final questions, or even discuss them with a friend. There's also a study guide at the end of *Sacred Refuge* that is perfect for small groups—or for simply digging deeper on your own.

> ## Together we will move from *finding* sacred refuge, to *abiding* in God's refuge, to *sharing* his refuge with others.

Sacred refuge is God's blood-bought gift to us in Christ. It is where we discover abundant life, peace, love, forgiveness, belonging, joy, provision, and every other good gift God has for us. But here's the catch: refuge is most often found when God allows crisis in our lives. Is it because he's cruel and capricious? The enemy would try to tell us so. But don't fall for that deception. It's the evil one's attempt to rip you off from the riches God has for you in dark times.

Right in the middle of our crises, God is extending us a holy invitation. Even now, if you listen very carefully, you may hear his voice asking you these questions:

> *What if the deepest desire of your heart turned out to be what I most long to give you? What if your crisis turned out to be the means through which you receive it?*

Writing this book turned out to be a living laboratory in which God challenged me to road test its truths. *Is God really good? Does he really see or care about me? Can he protect me, heal me, provide for me?* These are a few of the questions addressed in *Sacred Refuge*. And God answered them for me with a resounding "Yes!" It's the same answer he gave to our sacred sisters throughout the Bible. My prayer is that you, too, will discover (or perhaps rediscover) the heart of a God who loves you with tender affection, surrounds you with fierce protection, and longs to give you refuge under the shelter of his wings.

He is all we have.

He is all we need.

PART ONE

Finding Sacred Refuge

As Dorothy so eloquently put it: "Toto, I have a feeling we're not in Kansas anymore." We don't have to look far to see that Dorothy was right. Political divisiveness, economic uncertainty, and cultural upheaval make us want to run for cover. Add to that the personal crisis you are navigating right now, and your heart cries out, "Where is the safe place I need?"

Moses found it in the cleft of the rock as God passed before him in glory. Hannah experienced it as God promised her a child. Elijah discovered refuge from fear as God spoke to him in a still, small voice on Mt. Horeb. But is it possible, you wonder, to find rest and peace for *yourself*?

In the first three chapters of *Sacred Refuge*, we'll meet biblical women who found this place of shelter for their souls. Like you, they wrestled with questions such as "Can God restore what's been broken?" "Can God make a way forward from here?" "Can God free me from the shame of my sin?" Know this: just as he was with these sacred sisters in their crisis, God is with you in yours. But what is the path to this deep "soul sigh" we all long for?

Several years ago, I came across a photo of a mother bird sheltering two babies under her wings. The image went viral on social media because it displayed what our hearts most long for in uncertain days: a safe place. The way to this refuge is the practice of seeking God. The psalmist addressed our longing with this stunning promise: "He who dwells in the shelter of the Most High will abide in the shadow of the Almighty" (Psalm 91:1).

God is passionately committed to helping you find your safe place in him. Will you, by faith, step out and say to the Lord, "My refuge and my fortress, [you are] my God, in whom I trust" (Psalm 91:2)? Sister, will you come find refuge under his wings?

(CHAPTER 1)

Loved

Finding Shelter in the Promised Savior

How precious is your steadfast love, O God!
The children of mankind take refuge in the
shadow of your wings.

—Psalm 36:7

Can God restore what's been broken?

WEARING A PLAID jumper and scuffed Mary Jane shoes, at four years old, I stood rooted to a spot on the swirling green carpet as I watched my father walk out the front door of our apartment. I was sure everything good in my life was leaving with him.

Standing with my face pressed to the window as his form receded into the distance, I reasoned, *If my father, who is supposed to love me, leaves me, that must mean I'm not worth staying for.*

The enemy of my soul lost no time leveraging this colossal rejection to his advantage. My young ears heard, "You're nothing and no one."

The words eviscerated me before I knew what *eviscerated* meant, emptying my heart of worth and identity. The enemy's lies sucked the life from my lungs. For years afterward, I felt like I couldn't quite catch my breath.

Sensing his advantage—as all vile predators do—the enemy pressed in: "And the best you can hope for is to fake everyone out. Build a life on the outside that looks good, and maybe someone will think you're something after all."

I grasped for the straw offered me—I would control others' reaction to me by becoming perfectly unrejectable. In that moment my life shifted onto a foundation of fear based on my uneven performance. It was Eve's dilemma in Genesis 3. I fell for the lie that I had to *do* something, in order to *have* something, in order to *be* something.[1] Can you relate?

Heartbroken and deceived, I made a life-altering, unholy vow: "I will never let anyone reject me again." And God help me, I didn't.

Trying to control my own life would cost my freedom as I focused every ounce of energy on performing, pleasing, and proving. It meant my true self would go into hiding from God and others for years. It meant living in constant fear of what would happen if I didn't keep measuring up.

Sister, that's the price we pay for trying to be our own saviors.

Fortunately, God never stops pursuing us—even when we've gone into hiding. Eight years after my dad left, Jesus, the promised Savior, came for me. And when he did, my hiding days were numbered.

I was twelve. My mother had remarried, and we were running a ski resort in the White Mountains of New Hampshire.

One Sunday night, after all the weekend skiers had left, my mother and I were alone in the resort's lobby watching Dr. Billy Graham, who was preaching about the Samaritan woman of John 4. First, Dr. Graham broke the bad news: I had a sin problem that separated me from a holy God.

As I sat there thinking about my offenses, I knew I had no means to make amends on my own. Even at twelve, I realized that though I could fool everyone else, God knew the state of my heart. And it wasn't pretty.

But then the good news of the gospel broke over my heart like a wave of living water. That night I encountered a God who loved me enough to pursue me. My heavenly Father's pursuit of me began to undo the damage done to my heart when I watched my earthly father leave. I was surrounded with a growing sense of God's love that called me—for the first time—out of hiding.

Since my dad's abandonment, I had lived in a place of fear, constantly expecting rejection. But on this night, in a life-altering encounter with the presence of God, I knew I was safe. The Holy Spirit gave me the ability to believe, for the first time, that there was something in me Jesus valued and loved. I knew that despite my inability to produce anything of lasting value on my own, he valued me as I am. Jesus died in my place because he loves me.

He had come for me, and as the Holy Spirit worked, I trusted that Jesus was my bridge from sin and shame into the Father's arms of love and acceptance. With just-birthed faith, I stepped out of hiding and into the shelter of his arms.

Pursued out of Hiding

What makes you feel like hiding right now? If this season of your life had a vocabulary list, you might be rehearsing words like *frustration, betrayal, disappointment, disbelief, overwhelm, concern, anxiety*. And, underneath them all, *fear*. Not hard words to spell or define. But words that are hard to voice and even harder to swallow.

You may not be sure how you got here. You were the good girl, one of the church or neighborhood "dependables," going about your business (or was that *busyness*?). Doing all the things. Running VBS. Teaching Sunday school or children's church or ESL classes for foreign refugees. Volunteering for the least appealing positions for the fundraising benefits. Serving the marginalized in your community. Tutoring underserved kids. Homeschooling your kids. Giving generously. And now this? This is not what you expected after trying so hard to follow and please God.

The crisis you now face has left you feeling like a fawn trying to find her footing on an icy pond. Fear gnaws at your spirit, nibbling away unseen in the dark. What form has it taken? Fear of death or loss or destitution? Fear of rejection, of failure, or even of success? Fear of the future? Fear for your children's future?

The incident (or incidents) has turned life upside down. Nothing is the same—schedules, routines, relationships. Amid the tumult, you may be questioning God, feeling like he has forgotten you as you stagger under the weight of this strange new reality.

Take heart, my sister. You're not forgotten or alone.

To the exiles of Israel, God spoke these words through the prophet Isaiah: "Can a mother forget the baby at her breast and have no compassion on the child she has borne? Though she may forget, I will not forget you! See, I have engraved you on the palms of my hands" (Isaiah 49:15–16 NIV).

God's care for us is even greater than that of a loving, faithful parent, deeper than that of a newborn's mother. What if, in the pain of your crisis, God is offering you an unexpected gift? What if hidden under all the overwhelming bills and junk mail that have come with this season of suffering, he has sent an engraved invitation for you to encounter him as you never have before?

Where's the evidence?

That's what we're here to talk about. And we can find it in the earliest pages of our sacred story.

Eve's Story

To discover how Jesus restores the abandoned, broken, and hopeless, let's go back to the place where unholy fear was birthed and humanity's battle began. Since the moment after the fall—when Eve and then Adam chose to listen to a voice other than God's—we have experienced the consequences of trying to run our own lives. Eyes now wide-open, we know we are in trouble. Fear descends, acidic, into our bowels.

It feels like hiding is our only recourse. Soon control, fear's companion, sets up shop in our spirits, droning its unholy mantra: "It's all up to you. It's not safe to relinquish control of your life into God's hands. He's not good. He's not trustworthy."

Is there hope?

For those of us who know Jesus, there is great hope. He alone can answer our heart's cry from the vortex of crisis: *Can God really restore what's been broken?*

Reading the Bible's account of creation in Genesis is like watching a master watercolorist at work. The Artist spreads water evenly across a massive canvas. At just the right moment, he strokes swaths of rose, apricot, and gold onto the page, and shimmering color erupts across the top—the first sunrise. To the left he brings in azure, cerulean, and rich sapphire, the colors heaving, breaking, and shimmering into soft green and white foam—and the sea is born. In the center, the Artist dapples terra cotta hues, loamy browns, and vibrant greens—and the first garden sprouts forth from the ground.

For those of us who know Jesus, there is great hope. He alone can answer our heart's cry from the vortex of crisis.

Then, in the middle of it all, the Artist creates two figures, alike yet different. Man and woman, Adam and Eve. They are made for each other and for the Creator who has crafted this perfect paradise for them and their progeny. They live in this garden paradise in perfect harmony with their Creator, enjoying deep fellowship and unbroken communion with him. In this perfect relationship, they are fully seen, deeply known, and unconditionally loved by him. Adam and Eve are living out heaven on earth. All is well, throbbing with life and joy and fullness.

But then we read this phrase as Genesis 3 opens: "Now the serpent was more crafty than any of the wild animals the LORD God had made" (v. 1 NIV).

It is as if someone comes along and releases one drop of India ink into the middle of the Artist's splendid, color-splashed masterpiece. Instantly, black blots out the beauty that once lived in that spot. Slowly, almost imperceptibly, the black ink begins to seep into other parts of the picture until, eventually, all of it is marred.

Though we can discover how it happened by reading Genesis 3, if we could hear about it from Eve's unique perspective, she might tell us something like this:

Adam and I had a perfect life together before . . . before it wasn't. Father provided all that we needed and more. How we loved walking through his creation with him, delighting in each day's new discoveries. We talked together as Father and children, with a deep affection and knowledge of each other. Our lives were bathed in light, imbued with love.

One day as Adam and I were on our own near the edge of the garden, a serpent approached me. As soon as it opened its mouth and began to speak, that should have been our first clue that something was wrong. Really wrong. We should have run to Father. But we didn't.

It asked me a question and piqued my interest. Oh, how I wish I had turned away from its malevolent presence!

The serpent asked me, "Did God actually say, 'You shall not eat of any tree in the garden'?"

Hooked, I told him, "We may eat of the fruit of the trees in the garden, but God said, 'You shall not eat of the fruit of the tree that is in the midst of the garden, neither shall you touch it, lest you die.'"

It was as if a chilling breeze blew through me with the serpent's next words: "You will not surely die." Seeing he had our attention, he pressed in for the death blow: "For God knows that when you eat of it your eyes will be opened, and you will be like God, knowing good and evil."

The words hung in the air. They seemed to imply, "There is more. There is something that you are missing. And Father isn't offering it to you."

I thought to myself, *Yes, life is good. I am happy in this garden home with Adam and our Father. But I wonder if there is more. Perhaps I can be in control, as Father God is. If so, I want that.* I looked at the tree in the middle of the garden. The forbidden tree. Ah, how lovely it was. And its delectable fruit. Could it really make me wise and give me secret knowledge that Father had? I was hungry for that. *Well,* I thought, *why not?*

I took its fruit and also gave some to Adam. He didn't say a word, so I reasoned it must be all right. We each ate the fruit. Oh, how foolish we were!

Immediately, it was as if the sun lost its light. The earth beneath our feet shuddered. The trees around us swayed wildly in protest and pain. Adam and I looked at each other and knew we were naked.

Now exposed as disobedient children, we rushed to cover ourselves. Something—anything—would do. We found large fig leaves, but what good are fig leaves when shame is all you know, all you can feel?

Just then we heard Father walking among the trees. He was pursuing us, his disobedient children. And we were still not covered. We did all we knew to do. We hid. Deep in the underbrush of the trees, we waited, holding our breath.

Father called for Adam: "Where are you?" Shaking, Adam replied, "I heard the sound of you in the garden, and I was afraid, because I was naked, and I hid myself."

Father asked, "Who told you that you were naked? Have you eaten of the tree of which I commanded you not to eat?"

For the first time, Adam turned on me in cruel blame. Speaking to Father, he replied, "The woman whom you gave to be with me, she gave me fruit of the tree, and I ate."

Then came the worst moment of my life. Cowering in shame before Father, I heard his voice cry out in anger and heartache, "What is this that you have done?" All I could do, amid sobs of sorrow, was say, "The serpent deceived me, and I ate."

Eating the fruit seemed such a promising adventure—until

we ended up lost in a place we did not recognize, with no map to get home.

Father then turned to the serpent and pronounced a curse on that creature. Adam and I listened, still crouching and huddling in fear.

> ## Eating the fruit seemed such a promising adventure—until we ended up lost in a place we did not recognize, with no map to get home.

That's when I heard the words I will never forget. In the middle of Father's curse upon the serpent, he said: "I will put enmity between you and the woman, and between your offspring and her offspring; he shall bruise your head, and you shall bruise his heel."

The moment we heard Father speak about this war that would be waged between our children and those of the serpent, something stirred deep within us. It felt like Father had covered us with a blanket. As he spoke, we experienced a pinprick of light piercing the dark void now surrounding us. With each word of his promise, the pinprick grew and enveloped us. Light. Hope. A future for us and our children beyond this overwhelming darkness.

Father promised a child who would come from Adam and me. A child whose heel would be bruised by the serpent; but in the bruising, Father said, the child would crush the serpent's head. The light grew within us. And one day, the darkness caused by us and by the serpent would be replaced by this light. We clung to this hope as a lifeline that would one day bring us back into the relationship we once had with Father.

In time, we came to realize that Father did not destroy us that day because he loved us so deeply. He had sought us out, pursued us, because he was committed to our good. He banished us from the garden so that we would never eat of the tree of life and so prolong the misery we had brought upon ourselves and our world. And he gave us a promise because he wanted us one day to come home.

Father's promise that all would one day be restored became a covering for us. Better than fig leaves or even the skins he provided, his promise became a shelter for our shattered hearts when life got hard (and it did).

Adam knew Father's words would come true. Trusting that light, he named me Eve, or "the mother of all living." And on the painful but joyful day I gave birth to our first child, I remembered Father's promise and named him Cain, which means "I've got him." How I hoped this child would be the one to fulfill Father's promise to us!

Later, long after Father clothed us with skins and banished us from our home with him in the garden, we carried the light of his promise within our minds and hearts. It sustained us, a strong and steady presence, all our days.

YOU MIGHT BE HIDING IF . . .

It's easy for us to envision Adam and Eve hiding and assume it was their isolated issue—but is it? As we'll see in these pages, many women in Scripture hid in fear, desperation, shame, hopelessness, self-effort, loss, heartache, isolation, and distraction. What about us?

If you can relate to any of the following statements, it might indicate that you're in hiding.

- You show a different face/persona based on where you are at any given time.

- You can't remember the last time you felt true joy.
- You feel like you're living someone else's life, not the one you chose or were called to.
- You have the strange sensation of going through the motions.
- You struggle with tasks that require creativity.
- You edit what you say and do on a regular basis.
- You don't let people into your inner life, including your struggles, fears, or pain.
- Your days are full of striving, but you're not sure where you're headed.
- Your thoughts regularly return to fear or shame.
- Almost no one knows who you really are.
- You can't think of the last time you just sat down with God and poured your heart out to him.

If you find yourself in this "hiding" list, resist the temptation to hide even further behind a curtain of denial! This is your God-given moment, sister, to pay attention to the invitation God is offering you.

Called out of Hiding

Do your own fears sometimes push you into hiding—from God or others, or even yourself? You will never experience the sacred refuge God offers by continuing to hide. Even now, the Father is offering you a relationship with him through Jesus Christ, the Savior promised to Adam and Eve. *He* is the Shelter. *He* is the safe place, and there is no other. If you've never received this gift, you can do so now.

There are three important parts of coming out of hiding and coming home to God:

1. Admit that your life falls short of his holiness.
2. Believe that Jesus Christ went to the cross and died on your behalf to remove your sin and restore your relationship with the Father.

3. Commit your life into his hands. (For help praying through these
   steps, look for "Prayer for Entering Sacred Refuge for the First
   Time" on p. 236 in appendix B.)

Maybe you made this crucial transition from death to life many years
ago, but you still hide from God and others. Take heart. There is a way
forward. As Paul told the believers in Colossae, "Therefore, as you received Christ Jesus the Lord, so walk in him" (Colossians 2:6).

Coming out of hiding and entrusting ourselves to God isn't a one-
time decision, but an ongoing process of releasing control and resting
deeply in him. Faith has been defined this way: "Faith in Jesus Christ
is a saving grace, whereby we receive and rest upon him alone for salvation, as he is offered to us in the gospel."[2]

The verbs *receive* and *rest* light our way. Yes, we receive Jesus by
faith when we are saved, but depending on him is an essential and ongoing spiritual practice. Having received Jesus, we learn how to rest
deeply in what he has already done for us. We will continue to take the
steps of receiving and resting until we see Jesus face-to-face.

Sheltered by Jesus, the Promised Savior

Perhaps you're thinking, *This is all well and good, but what I am going
through at this moment is harder than anything I've ever experienced before. Everything within me feels like running and hiding from God. Can
he really restore what's been stolen in my life? Can I trust that he is ultimately for me and not against me?* In answer, let's fix our eyes on Jesus.

The beloved disciple, John, wrote these words in 1 John 3:8: "The
devil has been sinning from the beginning. The reason the Son of God
appeared was to destroy the works of the devil." One of the key verbs
in this passage is the Greek word *luo*, which can be translated as "destroy, undo, release, unbind, or set free." In the context of 1 John 3:7–
8, biblical scholars agree the verb means "to overthrow" or "do away
with." This is the powerful work Jesus accomplished through his rescue mission that signals the all clear to come out of hiding.

I remember touring a Nazi concentration camp in Poland some years ago. At one point we walked through the children's barracks. My fingers ran along the side of small wooden bunks that once held tiny bodies curled up against the cold. For those children who survived the war, I wonder what it was like for them the day Allied soldiers marched in to free survivors. I imagine there was boundless joy. Deep relief. A new beginning.

> **TRANSFORMING TRUTH**
>
> Fear tells you, "You are on your own." But God says, "Come out of hiding, beloved. I am here. And I will always love you."

Jesus's life, death, and resurrection undo the enemy's scheme to put us in permanent hiding, away from the sheltering presence of the One who loves us. As we trust God's promises, they will always prove stronger than our fears. Like neon pavers, they will lead us out of hiding in dark places. And what a beautiful freedom we will enjoy when we follow them!

Promised Triumph

The Father's promise of a Savior in Genesis 3:15 foreshadowed the ultimate showdown between Satan and Jesus Christ—played out on the cross of Calvary. There, Jesus fulfilled his purpose of overthrowing the works of the devil (1 John 3:8). How exactly was this strange promise involving bruised heels and crushed heads fulfilled?

Millennia before the invention of crucifixion as a means of execution, God's promise in Genesis 3:15 anticipated the moment when the serpent would "bite" the heel of Jesus Christ lifted up on the cross. In his sermon "The Excellency of Christ," the eighteenth-century preacher Jonathan Edwards provided this blow-by-blow account of how Jesus Christ destroyed the works of the destroyer:

> It was in Christ's last sufferings, above all, that he was delivered up to the power of his enemies; and yet by these, above all, he obtained victory over his enemies. . . . Christ never so

effectually bruised Satan's head as when Satan bruised his heel. The weapon with which Christ warred against the devil, and obtained a most complete victory and glorious triumph over him, was the cross, the instrument and weapon with which [Satan] thought he had overthrown Christ, and brought on him shameful destruction. . . . In his last sufferings, Christ sapped the very foundation of Satan's kingdom; he conquered his enemies in their own territories, and beat them with their own weapons.[3]

As stunning a victory as Jesus's resurrection was, he triumphed even further, ascending into heaven as a conquering King (Mark 16:19). Jesus's resurrection and ascension to the right hand of the Father were the final, crushing blow to the head of Satan. They demolished Satan's power to accuse, deceive, and destroy those who belong to God. They put the final nail in the final shingle of the unassailable shelter under which we now rest.

Does crisis still blindside us sometimes? Painfully so. But consider the words of Pastor Tim Keller, who died after a long bout with pancreatic cancer: "We know for certain, from Scripture and experience, that there are more dark times to come. And yet also more joy than we can now imagine."[4]

The picture the apostle John saw in Revelation included this stunning promise: "He will wipe away every tear from their eyes, and death shall be no more, neither shall there be mourning, nor crying, nor pain anymore, for the former things have passed away" (Revelation 21:4).

Know this, sister. There will come a day when all suffering, including yours, will cease. When all tears will stop flowing. If you are in Christ, your eyes will see God bring a full restoration of what has been stolen, killed, and destroyed by the enemy. On that day, the promised Savior will complete his work of annihilating the works of the devil. Then Revelation 21:5 will be wondrously fulfilled. We will hear the voice of the One who is seated on the throne say, "Behold, I am making all things new."

Promised Restoration

Remember how sin broke the connection with my earthly father when I was four? Years later, God moved in a powerful way to create something new in my relationship with my dad. Though the relationship was marred by a broken beginning, Jesus undid the work of the enemy in this important part of my life.

It happened at age nineteen, when I experienced a powerful renewal of my relationship with God. After I had discovered God's love for me at twelve, I struggled to live under Jesus's lordship. Hungry for male affirmation, I called the shots in my own life. By my first year in college, I was in a crisis of disobedience.

But God's Spirit wooed my heart to a place of repentance and forgiveness. The summer after my first year of college, I visited my dad. Because of the sheltering grace I received through Jesus, I was able to lovingly confront my earthly father and forgive him from my heart.

When that happened, my dad and I began a whole new relationship. In that important conversation—and the many others that followed—I watched Jesus undo the work of the devil. He began to reverse the effects of divorce and abandonment that had separated me from my dad and caused such a crisis in my heart. As the years passed, that healed relationship blossomed and I watched my dad come to Christ.

This moment of reconciliation was a gift from God—a snapshot of our promised Savior's power to restore what's been broken. And though we may not see every strained situation or relationship mended on this side of heaven, we know Jesus has already won the ultimate victory over Satan's schemes. Restoration will win, either here or in eternity.

Experiencing Jesus's Shelter

In the chapters ahead, we'll discover how God brings restoration to us as we turn to him for shelter. When we stop hiding and dwell with him, our hearts' deepest longings are fulfilled. Our desires to be loved and pursued, to be seen, forgiven, and healed. Our longings to be provided for, rescued, wooed, and empowered. Our yearning to be the beloved.

Sister, how do you most need to be sheltered at this moment? What would refuge look like for you?

Maybe you're overwhelmed by the demands that constantly scream for your attention as a mom and feel like all you do is fail. Maybe your heart has been shattered by a deep loss. You might be living in the past and going through the motions in the present. Or perhaps you've faded away from a once-close relationship with God but haven't a clue if he still wants anything to do with you.

Will you let the story of God's mercy to Adam and Eve encourage you? When all hell breaks loose and the enemy tries his best to steal, kill, or destroy, God holds wide the door of refuge in the promised Savior, Jesus Christ. It's what God did for Eve. It's what he provided when the enemy waged war against me, not with mortar shells and bullets, but with the same weapon of deception he used against Eve.

And it's what he's offering to you too.

Enter the Sacred Refuge of God's Love

Perhaps Jesus is encouraging you right now with words like these:

I see you, beloved one. I know the effects of the fall have left you battered and beaten. Life has been so harsh, the losses so great, the pain so severe. And now this crisis threatens to undo you.

You have done what you knew to do: you have hidden. Tucked up in the back of a cave, you sit in the dark. Cold and alone, you are more than a little afraid. Your heart is saying, *Life has been too hard. I don't think I can trust God. It feels safer just to hide out here for a while.*

Beloved, I know what it's like to be where you are. I lay in a cave many years ago, alone in the dark. I was as dead as you feel right now. But even as I fulfilled the Father's promise to send a Savior, the Father kept his promise to me. He sent the Spirit to breathe new life into my breathless body. And I arose. I walked out of that cave in glorious power and into my full inheritance as the conquering Lord.

Know this: The same power that raised me from the dead is available to you right now. To help you begin to breathe again. To allow light to pierce your darkness. To lift you up and help you take that crucial first step out of the cave and toward me, your true home.

I know your life right now isn't what you expected. But instead of pivoting away from me and into deeper isolation, accept my invitation to let the pain you are feeling propel you toward me. I will be your safe place, beloved.

On the cross I undid the work of the enemy. I have come to undo the destruction he has wreaked in your life. I have come to restore what has been taken from you.

Let us begin with fear, which has stolen so much from you. What are you most afraid of, beloved? Let fear's oppressive mantle fall from your shoulders. Yes, push it off and let it stay in the cave where it belongs. My perfect love displaces fear. Let me surround you with my liquid love, enveloping and protecting you.

And your pain. Will you release it to me? I can hold the pain when it threatens to overwhelm you. Yes, that's it. Let it seep out, a caustic stream, from your heart into mine. It will not undo me, the man of sorrows, well-acquainted with grief. Beloved, in place of your sadness, I give you my comfort. Let the healing balm of my Spirit's presence flow right now into your damaged heart. Do you perceive that the healing work has begun?

How I love you and long to comfort you. Here, in the shelter of my arms, is the place you were created to live. Abiding peace and deep rest are here in this refuge I have built for you. I alone am your truly safe place. Will you stand up and trust that my love will hold you as you move toward me, your heart's true shelter? Arise, my love, my beautiful one. Will you take that first step toward home in my sacred refuge?[5]

REST Under His Wings

Quiet yourself in God's presence.

Release control.

1. What is happening in your life right now that causes you to fear? Do those fears ever lead you to try controlling people or situations in your life? If so, what areas have you tried to control?

Father, I have hidden from you in the fear that you are not in control (so I need to be). Forgive me, please, and help me to believe that you have all things—perfectly, wisely, and lovingly—in hand.

Exchange your old *fears* for the shelter of Jesus's *love*.

2. Have your fears caused you to hide from God or others? Did you find yourself in the list on page 35?
3. How has hiding affected your relationship with Jesus? Write a prayer, pouring out your heart to him about the state of your relationship, and what you hope it can become.
4. Which of God's promises do you find most encouraging right now? How can it help you exchange your fear for God's shelter?

See yourself in union with Christ.

5. What would it look like for you to pivot away from your fears and toward the light of Christ's shelter—his constant, loving presence with you?

Father, I relinquish control of my life into your loving hands. With my eyes on Jesus, I trust that you have provided all I need to come out of hiding and into the shelter of your love. Help me now to take that first step.

Trust Christ as your promised Savior.

6. In what ways have you struggled to trust God?

Father, you know all the reasons I struggle to trust you. In trying to control things, I have made a huge mess, and I am done. Please give me grace to trust you with each person, relationship, and situation. I am willing to come out of hiding; help my unwillingness.

7. Create a "breath prayer." This is a short form of prayer in which we speak the first part of the prayer as we inhale and the second part of the prayer as we exhale. For example, try inhaling as you say, "Father," and exhaling with the words "help me." Other options are "Father . . . I need you" or "Jesus . . . I trust you." You can pray this breath prayer moment by moment as you continue to walk out of hiding and into God's sheltering presence.

CHAPTER 2

Known

Finding Shelter in the One Who Sees You

Let me dwell in your tent forever!
Let me take refuge under the shelter of your wings!
—PSALM 61:4

Can God make a way forward from here?

CRISIS HAS A way of making us feel invisible to others. It saps our hope and makes us feel like we are standing one inch away from a brick wall. But God meets us even there.

Rhoda experienced God's presence amid the ongoing crises of her childhood. She lived with her parents, sister, and brother on a subsistence farm. Being the eldest, she was given a lot of responsibility because her mother worked outside the home. Rhoda tried to look after her siblings as best she could, and she was also given the regular tasks of milking and caring for the livestock they raised to slaughter and sell.

Rhoda told me that she has few vivid memories of her childhood, but from about the ages of eleven to fifteen, she recalls being physically, verbally, and sexually abused. She would often run away to the southernmost part of her farm to escape.

One day Rhoda followed a small woodland stream that ran the length of the south forty. And that's where she found her refuge. In that stream was a large, absolutely smooth table rock, about the size of a small bed with a slightly higher area toward one end. (In her mind, that formation seemed like a sailboat that helped her escape her troubles.) Lying there, Rhoda felt safe and secure. There was no similar stone or rock formation anywhere in the vicinity. It looked as if a glacier had carried it for many miles, perfectly smoothing and shaping it, and placing it right where she would need it.

Near the stone was a small spring that bubbled out from the hill, surrounded by fern and moss—cool even on a hot, humid day. The water had shaped a basin in the rock by swirling little stones around in it over time. Rhoda still remembers the refuge she found in that special place—a space where she felt seen by God:

> I can still see it in my mind, a rare memory. I believe my refuge in the woods was a gift from my heavenly Father. It was a place I visited repeatedly because I felt sheltered there. In every other part of my life, I felt unseen and invisible. But in the sanctuary God gave me, I felt safe. In that place I had the sense God was near me, he saw me, and he cared about me. Quite simply, my rock by the stream enabled me to survive.

Rhoda had abundant reasons to feel despair. Her young life was shaped by grueling work and heartbreaking abuse. And no one around her seemed to notice or care. But she discovered that God saw her and had compassion on her. Turning to him for refuge made all the difference.

Longing to Be Seen

Sister, what's your dead end right now? What is the place you have wandered to that feels like you're exiled from your true self and abundant life? Where are you feeling pulled toward hopelessness and despair?

You're not alone. Lots of us wake up each morning to a life we didn't sign up for. We trudge through our days and cry over our coffee, "Oh, God, how did I end up here?" At such moments it's easy to miss the sacred refuge God is offering us in Jesus. Thinking it's up to us to solve our problems, we fix our eyes on our own ability to change things. We miss his cues; we are blind to his invitations.

This idea of being seen, as Rhoda was by God, may be a new one for you. Growing up, I often felt unseen. Then in late high school something shifted in my life. I went from being the gangly ugly duckling, unnoticed and unseen, to someone with the power to attract attention. (Not always good attention, but that's another story.) I remember the euphoria that came with that power.

But what about when time takes its toll on our appearance? Or what if we have never possessed that power? Is there a way of being seen that has nothing to do with flawless skin or long, flowing tresses?

YOU ARE NOT ALONE

It's happened so many times I've lost count. I'll be teaching a retreat and a woman will ask to speak with me privately. Or someone I'm meeting for coffee will suddenly open up about how hard her life has gotten. At some point, I'll hear these words: "I just feel so alone. I could make it through if I knew someone else was with me in this."

Sister, here's the best news you may ever hear: In spite of the enemy's desire to isolate and pick you off, and despite the ever-quickening pace of life that pulls us away from each other through the centrifugal force of busyness, God says this to you: "Beloved, you are not alone. I am here. Right here. Right now. I am with you in this crisis. And I am leading you to a place of deep rest and safety."

Remember, this is the God who:

- pursued Adam and Eve and their errant children in love;
- initiated the covenant of grace with Abraham that forged an unbreakable bond between God and his people—forever;
- called the Israelites out of slavery in Egypt, out of bondage to false gods, and into abundant life with him; and
- called Joshua to lead the children of Israel into the Promised Land, and promised, "I will be with you. I will not leave you or forsake you" (Joshua 1:5).

Why did he do all this? Because he longed to have a relationship with them—and he wants the same with us.

The most astounding proof of God's commitment to always be with us is Jesus. God broke into our world as a flesh-and-blood human to buy back his rebel sons and daughters. He did it out of love for us. He did it so we would never live a day—here or in eternity—apart from his loving presence.

This is the God who invites you to enter his sacred refuge. Regardless of how lost, forgotten, or marginalized you may feel at this moment, let Jesus's words resonate powerfully in your spirit: "And behold, *I am with you always*, to the end of the age" (Matthew 28:20, emphasis added).

Sister, if you're wondering if there is a way of being known that goes deeper than the images we see splashed across our screens, I have good news for you. There is.

We don't have to create a false online persona or pretend we are more than we are to attract God's attention—his eye is always on us. Too often, though, we lose sight of that constant presence amid our everyday cares. But when life brings us to the end of ourselves and to a place where we are at an impasse, that's exactly where we can experience the depth of being known by God. At that moment, when our forlorn hearts cry out, "God, can you make a way forward from here?" he reveals himself as the One who sees us and creates a path in the deserts of our lives.

Hagar's Story

God offered this kind of deep and hopeful knowing in the life of a tent-dweller named Hagar. She had sought refuge in her youth and fertility, but neither of those were enough to protect her when her life blew up. Hagar's story unfolds in Genesis 16 and 21 (though we will focus on chapter 16). Take a few minutes to read about this sister who suffered—but found solace in the One who saw her as no one else could.

If Hagar could tell us her story, it might sound something like this:

I should have known there would be trouble when Abram, Sarai, and their caravan rolled into our city in Egypt. They were older and clearly favored by the gods. Abram walked like a pharaoh, sure-footed and stately. And Sarai? She was a stunner. Turning everyone's head with her beauty and grace, she ended up in the house of Pharaoh himself, purported to be Abram's sister.

"My sister," my eye. Everyone but Pharaoh himself suspected the truth. So when the boils began, first with Pharaoh's household, then with the palace servants, it didn't take long to figure out why the gods were angry.

Me? I was just a commodity, Pharaoh's parting gift to Sarai, the woman whose beauty—even in old age—got us all into a world of mess. Sure, Abram and Sarai walked out of Egypt with extra flocks, silver, gold, and me. But I lost my home, my family, and all that was familiar as I joined this strange group from Ur on their way to who knew where.

I was just a commodity. I lost my home, my family, and all that was familiar.

I was Sarai's lady's maid, answerable to her, but in reality I felt more like a slave—unable to speak up for myself. Sarai was the mistress, and everything revolved around her. I was mostly unseen and unheard.

It didn't take long before I heard about the encounter Abram had with his god. There was something about a promise. Children as numerous as the stars. A nation that would inherit a rich land. And it all hinged on an heir.

From the beginning, I wondered why Abram and Sarai didn't have children. As her personal servant, I can tell you it wasn't from lack of trying. But month after month, I watched as Sarai's bleeding returned. I saw her bitter tears, heard her crying softly into her pillow late at night. I saw how the whole camp waited to hear news of a child on the way. I witnessed the shame Sarai bore as barrenness stole her status and worth. Who wouldn't feel sorry for her?

So when we had been in Canaan ten years and still there was no child in Sarai's belly, no heir for Abram's growing riches, who was I to refuse Sarai's brilliant idea?

Late one night I overheard her talking to Abram: "The Lord has prevented me from bearing children. Go in to my servant; it may be that I shall obtain children by her." Oh, it was a common enough practice in the day, but it rarely turned out well for anyone. Still, I reasoned, it could be my ticket to another kind of life. From obscure servant to second wife and mother of the heir? It might not be such a bad idea, at that.

After only two or three months with Abram (who was kind enough), I was with child. The news traveled fast throughout the camp, and we all rejoiced.

But the happiness was short-lived. When the knowledge bloomed in me that I had achieved in short order what had eluded my mistress for decades, my heart grew bold. I, not Sarai, had the power to bear life, to give Abram the heir he longed for. I felt special, favored, and entitled to brag.

People whispered about me as I walked by. They treated me differently. Sure, I had been the invisible servant for years, but now I was somebody. And it felt oh, so good.

I paid bitterly for it, but at the time, each of my snide comments and sideways smirks at Sarai's expense was delicious to me. "Take that. And that," my heart said to my mistress. I knew it stung her, but it was as if every indignity I had suffered rose up within me and would not be silenced. And so I let her have a taste of what it felt to be the outsider.

However, it all blew up the day I stood before Sarai as she sat on the ground repairing a corner of our tent. As I purposefully

stretched in front of her, my growing belly protruding trium-
phantly in her face, she snapped. Sarai went to Abram and
complained about my contempt for her. I quickly learned that
even my pregnancy—and the future heir who grew inside
me—wasn't enough to protect me from Abram's frustrated,
"Do to her as you please!"

Given that permission, Sarai laid into me, dishing back all
I had given to her, and then some. Life became unbearable.
Withholding food from me, screaming at me, treating me like
less than a slave—Sarai had her revenge.

One morning, as I was emptying her bed pot at the edge
of the camp, I looked out at the expanse of the desert before
me. Quiet. Clean, open space. No more drama. And a possible
road back to my home in Egypt. I dropped the pot and never
looked back.

My destination was Shur, near the northeastern border of
Egypt. Several miles into the wilderness, I realized I should
have planned better. I was young and strong, but the desert
was no place for a woman, let alone a woman in my condition.

Within a day or two, my thirst brought me to the end of
myself. Somehow, I made it to a spring of water and drank my
fill. But I had no food. It was just a matter of time before wild
dogs put an end to me. Filled with despair, I lay down to die
and wept bitterly.

Imagine my surprise when I realized someone was there
with me. At first I felt relief. Perhaps this person had food and
could bring me to Egypt. But when I stirred from my resting
place near the stream and looked up, my relief turned to fright.

A being filled with light was standing before me, looking
directly at me. His gaze was like fire.

Then a voice arose from him sounding like the surge of
many waters: "Hagar, servant of Sarai, where have you come

from and where are you going?" The voice carried both authority and compassion.

How did he know my name? I had the uneasy (yet also comforting) sense that he knew everything about me.

And how did he know I had been Sarai's servant? Who was this? And why had he come? I wanted to burrow into the sand and disappear, but there was no hiding from this being who was light and life and love.

Finally, I responded, "I am fleeing from my mistress Sarai." All I knew to do in that moment was speak the truth.

Then I heard the words I least wanted to hear: "Return to your mistress and submit to her." My stomach churned. Why would I go back to where my pride had created a mess with such hard consequences? It was so much easier to run.

Then I looked out over the expanse of the desert before me, stretching for miles. I realized I didn't know where I was going. I had no plan, no protection, no future. Hopelessness crept into my spirit. I would die here. My baby would never come into the world. I was sitting at a dead end at the back of beyond.

But at that place of utter desolation, I encountered an unexpected place of safety. A seed of hope fell into the fertile soil of my desperation and began to grow.

As if he had read my mind, the being spoke words that fell like spring rain on tender shoots: "I will surely multiply your offspring so that they cannot be numbered for multitude . . . Behold, you are pregnant and shall bear a son. You shall call his name Ishmael, because the Lord has listened to your affliction. He shall be a wild donkey of a man, his hand against everyone and everyone's hand against him, and he shall dwell over against all his kinsmen."

He made such promises! He said that the Lord himself had listened to my affliction. Was it possible that he was Jehovah, the God I had heard Abram and Sarai speak of? Who was I to experience this visitation? Who was I to receive such promises from him about the child quickening even then in my belly?

A son. I would bear a son. And I was to call him Ishmael, which means "God hears." What a gift! Every time I called his name, I would be reminded of the compassion of this God-man who was covering me with a blanket of hope.

At that place of utter desolation, I encountered an unexpected place of safety.

Having grown up in Egypt, I thought there were many gods. They were immortal but impersonal. I never dreamed there was one God, or that this One was personal, knowable. But seeing the God-man made it all clear. He had always been there. Had always had his eye upon me.

I never saw this coming. I had been unseen in Egypt, a throwaway. I had been unseen by Abram, simply a receptacle for seed and a means to an end. I had been unwanted in Sarai's eyes when what filled my womb became a threat.

But this One. This God-man had heard my cry in the wilderness. He pursued me and saw me in my distress. He responded because he cared deeply about what happened to me and my child. And he made a way forward for us both.

I sat up straighter from my position on the ground. As I heard the words from the God-man's mouth, I knew they carried divine authority. What he decreed would indeed come to pass. There was a hope and a future for both me and my baby.

Filled with a fresh wind of encouragement, I dared to look at the One before me. "You are El Roi," I said. "You are the God who sees me" (and the God I see).

I was not divine, and he was not human. But at the stream in the desert, I entered a refuge that I took back with me on the long road home to Abram and Sarai.

I had been seen, and I would never be unseen again.

Seeing the One Who Sees Us

Maybe you can relate to Hagar in her desert wilderness. Your life has been turned upside down, and you are running for cover. Or perhaps, like Rhoda from the beginning of this chapter, you've been fleeing from those who hurt you (or those whom you have hurt), and you have come to a dead end. You see no way forward, no way out, and hopelessness has set in. You feel isolated, unseen, and unknown.

At the moment when you feel most unseen, the God of the universe is showing up in mercy to fulfill his purposes for your life. He has come to enter your most vulnerable moment and build a powerful shelter for you. It's made of his presence, his ability to see and know you. It's made of his love for you and his intention to give you (and yours) a hope and a future. Will you let his love call you out of hiding?

It may be hard for some of us to relate to Hagar's situation. We live in homes with solid walls and strong roofs, filled with comforts and conveniences. But consider, if you will, the state of your heart. Is it possible that, like Hagar, you wake up each morning with a dull ache in an existence you don't know how you stumbled into? Life used to be better. It made more sense. A crisis you didn't see coming has hindered your heart from seeing and trusting God.

Feeling like a refugee in your own life, you have fled from everything that once felt safe and good and true. You find yourself alone, plodding through your days, wondering if there's a way forward from the dead end you have hit. You may have spent years quietly hiding in despair.

Just keep on keepin' on, you tell yourself. *Things will get better.*

But they don't—and it might be because your pride has kept you from repenting of your sin before God and others. Perhaps you hid when you feared being found out. Or maybe you hid because life felt hopeless and a good future was obscured from your view. You no longer had the strength to face God or the world.

When the consequences of bad decisions (ours or others') have left us with nowhere to go, Jesus's atoning work paves a clear path for us back to abundant life in the Father's house.

Like our sisters Rhoda and Hagar who found solace in the One who saw and knew them, you, too, can come out of hiding in despair. You can pivot back toward the God who offers to shelter you in his arms. There is sacred refuge for you there.

Sheltered by Jesus, Who Sees Us

Life can often feel like we have lost our way in a desert. Where can we find water? What will we eat? How do we get out of this unbearable sun? Where do we go from here?

The answers to all these questions, of course, are found in Jesus Christ, our perfect Shelter.

Pursued, Protected, and Promised a Future

The world we live in often urges us to worship our success or hopes we will fail. But God pursues us like a bodyguard who won't let us out of his sight. When we mess up, he offers us the safety of forgiveness and a fresh start. He pours his unconditional love into us. He keeps us safe and redirects us back to life and hope.

The apostle Paul put it this way in Romans 5:7–8: "For one will scarcely die for a righteous person—though perhaps for a good person one would dare even to die—but God shows his love for us in that while we were still sinners, Christ died for us." Consider that, sister. Even knowing you would go your own way, Jesus Christ considered your life worthy of his. He set out on history's greatest rescue mission—dying in your place. And now by the power of his Spirit, he is running after you in love.

Just as Jesus protects us from an eternity without God, he also protects us and shelters us here, day to day. In our coming and going. In our waking and sleeping. From attacks and alarms. Jesus wraps his fiercely protective love around us.

Sister, what situation are you facing right now that feels impossible? Where are you unable to see a happy ending or even light at the end of the tunnel?

Are you in union with Christ by faith? If so, "your life is hidden with Christ in God" (Colossians 3:3). From that place, God makes an extraordinary promise to you that only he has the power to fulfill. You've likely heard it or read about it in Romans 8:28: "And we know that for those who love God all things work together for good, for those who are called according to his purpose."

God is at work in all things. The bad stuff you've been running from, the painful stuff you'd do anything to avoid, even the mysteries you have no answers for. He has it all in hand, and he promises to work it together for your good—and that "good" is "to be conformed to the image of his Son" (v. 29).

When you can't see—he sees. And he's still faithful. Just as he did for Hagar, showing up in her mess to create a future for her and her family, he will do the same for you.

Seen on the Brink of Oblivion

I saw Jesus's loving protection firsthand in the life of a teen girl I met while teaching at a retreat. Just fifteen years old, Maddie was the kind of girl you wouldn't notice unless she tapped you on the shoulder.

Which is exactly what she did after my final talk of the weekend. As I was packing up my notes, Maddie asked me a question I knew was a cry for help.

"Let's take a walk, okay?" I offered.

"Sh-sure."

As I asked her about what was happening in her life, I heard stories that made my heart cry out, *Oh, God. Oh, God, help this girl. Give me your words. Give me something just for her that will bring her hope.*

And he did. When she confessed she had been thinking about ending her life, I envisioned Maddie trussed up in a tiny spot with a blank wall before her and no way to move to the right or the left.

We went to prayer. And through the power of his Holy Spirit, Jesus began to pursue her. She was in the presence of the One who knew and loved her. Her breathing began to slow. Her fear began to melt away. I prayed for God to protect her from the enemy's lies about her lack of worth. God brought Scripture to my mind that communicated how he saw her: precious, unique, beloved. Maddie's face began to change.

I encouraged her to seek ongoing help from a biblical counselor, and then the Lord reminded me of this promise for his people, which I shared with Maddie: "Behold I am doing a new thing; now it springs forth, do you not perceive it? I will make a way in the wilderness and rivers in the desert" (Isaiah 43:19).

The girl who walked with me to the dining hall for supper was changed. Maddie knew she had encountered the living God, the One who saw her and loved her and made a way forward for her.

Sheltered in God's Sight

Hagar called the angel of the Lord *El Roi*—"the God who sees me." What does it mean for you to be seen by God? To know that the Holy One sees you can be intimidating because you know you are not perfect, and your faults are on full display. But being seen by God can also be comforting, because nobody sees you the way God does. He sees you and he sees *through* you. But here is the amazing thing: he still loves you.

Perhaps you've spent your whole life pouring all your efforts into trying harder and achieving more. It's left you exhausted and empty, feeling like Hagar, abandoned in the middle of nowhere. But Jesus is as near as your next breath. In compassion he is calling you out of hiding and into the only safe place you will ever find or need—his loving embrace.

In his book *Gentle and Lowly*, Dane Ortlund puts it this way: "Let Jesus draw you in through the loveliness of his heart. This is a heart that . . . embraces the penitent with more openness than we are able to feel. It is a heart that walks us into the bright meadow of the felt love of God. It is a heart that drew the despised and forsaken to his feet in self-abandoning hope."[1]

Sister, it's so tempting to hide when you're feeling "despised and forsaken." The harshness or judgment of others might have you running for cover. Your own failures may keep you burrowing deep behind your regrets. Maybe you've been hiding for a long time, trying to control your life, and now it all seems to be unraveling. But nothing you've been running from can keep you from being seen and known by God. Don't stay in the dead end of despair. There is hope. If you'll only take that first brave step out of hiding, Jesus stands ready to shelter you with his love.

Enter the Sacred Refuge of the One Who Sees You

Jesus may be speaking something like this to you right now:

> Beloved, I see you there. Sitting in the dark. Feeling like you're up against a wall, with nowhere to go. Circumstances have tempted you to believe the lie that you are all alone. How you long to be seen and helped!
>
> But even at this moment, this apparent dead end, I see you.
>
> You thought the life you built through your own efforts was a mansion, a safe house. But look around, dear one. It's no more than a lean-to. You thought you were building on solid ground, but now that foundation is shaking under your

feet, and everything is collapsing beneath you. I invite you to leave the sinking sand and come build your life on my solid rock.

You thought you would find safety in a relationship with a man—any man. Or in the attention and rush of power that came from your youth and beauty. You grabbed at the chance to build a bright future for yourself. It all seemed so promising, but in the end it led you down a dark alley of despair.

I invite you to leave the sinking sand and come build your life on my solid rock.

Turn toward me, dear one. I am *pursuing* you as no other lover ever has. For I am the One who sees. In my compassion, I have seen you suffer, and I cannot stay silent any longer.

I am revealing myself to you. I am letting you see my face. Even now, can you see my fingerprints on your life? I am here, and I am wooing you.

I am *protecting* you. If going your own way led you into darkness, will you now trust that I am shining the light of my Word on your path? It will provide clear guidance on your way home to me.

"But it's been so long," you say. "I've been running my own life for so long that I can't remember the way back."

Take heart, beloved. I have already made the way home for you. It is paved with my righteousness, which you can stand on without fear of it giving way. Step by step, day by day, bring your old sin, your old life to me in humility. Confess your sin to me, knowing that it is already paid for. Let the burdens drop from your shoulders and feel a spring return to your step.

I am *promising* never to abandon nor forsake you. As you

leave the old behind, I invite you to turn and face me. Do you feel it? There is a seismic shift happening under your feet. It's a heavenly sign to you that I AM making all things new.

Beloved, I call you to repent of running from me. Come out of hiding. As you make your way into my embrace, into the house I have prepared for you, I have this final instruction as you leave the place you've been living: Turn off the lights. Lock the front door. You won't be going back there. And the key does not go under the mat. Throw it, as I have, into the sea of forgetfulness on your way to my house.

My Father and I have turned on the front porch light. It will help you find your way.

Even now, we see you. We have you in our sights, our hearts racing with anticipation. Beloved, this very moment we are running to embrace you and celebrate your homecoming.[2]

REST Under His Wings
Spend time quieting yourself in God's presence.

Release control.
1. List the areas of your life that have caused you to despair. Have you been hiding from God in these areas? Where has this brought you, sister?
2. God is inviting you to take stock of your life at this moment. How would you respond if he asked you, "Where have you been?" (i.e., "What has brought you to this place?") What if he asked you, "Where are you going?" (i.e., "Is the path before you leading to light and life, or more darkness and death?")

Exchange your *despair* for the shelter of Jesus's *presence* and *hope*.
3. How has hiding in despair affected your relationship with Jesus?
4. How could you invite God's nearness and compassion into the areas of despair that you listed above?

Father, I have hidden from you in despair, not believing that you really saw or cared about what has happened to me. I come to you now, recognizing that hopelessness is stealing my life and joy. Forgive me, please, and begin to shine light on a path out of this maze. Send your Holy Spirit to breathe new life and hope into my spirit.

See yourself in union with Christ.
5. Is God calling you to make a course correction today? What step might help you pivot out of hiding from God and into the shelter of El Roi, the God who sees you?
6. What feelings surface when you think about being fully known by God? Ask God to help you live in light of your union with Christ.

Father, I ask you to lift this hopelessness from me. With my eyes on Jesus, I trust that you have provided all I need to come out of hiding and into the shelter of your loving presence.

Trust Christ as the one who sees you.
7. Create a breath prayer response to God that you can use throughout your day to connect to the One who knows you best. You might try: "Jesus . . . I see you." Or "Your Word . . . is a lamp to my feet." Or "Lord . . . lead me home."

CHAPTER 3

Forgiven

Finding Shelter in Christ's Righteousness

In you, O Lord, do I take refuge;
let me never be put to shame;
in your righteousness deliver me!
—Psalm 31:1

Can God free me from the shame of my sin?

YEARS AGO, A friend told me she was having problems with her marriage. Week by week, month by month, discontent grew in Corinne's spirit until she was consumed with the tantalizing idea that she could somehow fix her marital discontent by flirting with an attractive guy she met at the gym.

As we talked one day, she suggested with a playful smile that there was nothing wrong with simply looking. Heartsick, I warned her of how easy it would be to go from looking, to longing, to lusting—to losing her marriage.

On the morning after her "harmless fling" turned into an affair, Corinne called me. Distraught over what she had done, she was terrified her actions would destroy her family.

My friend's experience echoed the warning of Proverbs 20:17: "Food gained by fraud tastes sweet, but one ends up with a mouth full of gravel" (NIV). Driven by an unholy hunger, she ran after "food gained by fraud" through a relationship outside marriage.

Corinne's path to destruction started with simple *distraction* ("Oh, it doesn't hurt to look") that turned into *deception* ("I need more than my husband is giving me. I deserve a little fun"), which then devolved into *despair* ("What have I done? I hate who I have become"). Once there, she despaired of ever returning to life before her adultery. Shame settled in her spirit and began its destructive work.

Although it was tempting to judge this friend, and to say, "I told you so," I knew better. By this time in my twenties, I recognized the warning signs of adultery in my own life.

Corinne's headlong descent into sin mirrored my own spiritual infidelity to Jesus.

It became a cautionary tale for me about the ways I "stepped out on" Jesus, taking his love for granted and cheating on him with other lovers such as affluence, others' good opinions, or performance. Sister, do you find yourself in a similar place?

Secrets and Shame

They say we are only as sick as our secrets. If so, then our culture is mired in a major health crisis. Worse than a global pandemic, more pernicious than cancer or heart disease, secret sins lie unseen and unconfessed in our spirits. They erode intimacy and steal joy from our relationship with God, others, and even ourselves. They send us scurrying for cover faster than we can say, "Shame on you!"

Shame is one of Satan's most potent weapons. He gets plenty of mileage out of it because even as believers we tend to dwell on our broken past and sinful decisions. We fear being found out by others and rejected for our failures.

But shame can only exist if we forget the gospel and who we are in Christ. We can begin to live shame-free as we preach the gospel to ourselves each day, reminding ourselves (and so silencing the enemy's accusations) of the grace and forgiveness that God has already given us in Christ.

Sister, what's the secret sin that's been hiding, silent and deadly, in the back corner of your spirit? Is it the closet drinking that you keep telling yourself you have "under control"? The emotional affair with someone at church or at work? Your salacious habit of gossiping about or judging others? Late-night online shopping that's breaking your budget? Are you ready to come out of hiding in shame?

LIES THAT BIND VERSUS TRUTHS THAT FREE

Though God's Holy Spirit convicts us of sin in our lives, he will never shame us with sin; Jesus has already removed it! But one of Satan's great deceptions is trying to make us confuse the enemy's voice of shame with God's voice of love. So how do we discern the difference?

Satan's voice always highlights our sin with the goal of making us feel condemned and shame-ridden. He entices us to hide our sin. The Holy Spirit's voice, by contrast, convicts of sin with the goal of turning us back toward God through repentance and restoration. Satan's voice accuses God of hating or rejecting us for our sin; God's voice invites us to step closer, release our sin, and receive the forgiveness Jesus has already purchased for us. The enemy binds us through lies; God gloriously frees us with the truth of who he has made us to be in Christ.

Here is a list of common lies Satan uses to make us feel ashamed and alone—and the truths that will set us free:

Lies that Bind	Truths that Free
Performance: "I am what I do. I have to get my act together."	**Resting in Christ's Righteousness:** "I am who God says I am in Christ: righteous." (Romans 3:21–22; Matthew 11:28–30)
Perfectionism: "Only perfect girls are loved."	**Living Free of Perfectionism:** "I am perfect and whole in Christ, loved and accepted by the Father through Christ." (Romans 8:1; Colossians 2:6–10)
Fear: "I am afraid (of rejection, failure, the future)."	**Resting in God's Love and Presence:** "God's love for me leaves no room for fear." (1 John 4:18; Romans 8:31–35; Zephaniah 3:14–17)
Shame/Condemnation: "What I've done is too serious for God to forgive."	**Freedom from Shame/Condemnation:** "There is no condemnation left for me because Jesus was condemned in my place." (Romans 8:1; 1 John 1:8–9)

Pain: "I'm hurting. I must have lost God's love."	Healing and Wholeness: "God is with me in my pain. His love and comfort are mine in Christ." (Joshua 1:5; Psalm 34:18; Isaiah 49:15)
Isolation: "I am all alone."	(Re)Connecting with God: "I am not alone. God is with me and promises never to leave me." (Joshua 1:5; Matthew 28:20; Romans 8:15-17, 35-39)

Sister, what has your secret sin's presence cost you? Intimacy with God, with your husband, or in your friendships? Has it caused the persistent voice of shame to attack your heart?

Make no mistake. Sin—and the shame attached to it—is a powerful weapon in the enemy's arsenal against you. He delights in how the thought of your sin can still make you cringe in shame and step into a shadowy hiding hole—away from the only One who can deal with it once and for all. But it's a weapon that can no longer prosper (Isaiah 54:17)!

Maybe you've been sitting on this rotten egg for years. Lately its stench has grown unmistakable and you feel a crisis coming. How much longer can you hide behind the lie, "If I am exposed, there is no protection for me"?

Maybe you've begun to wonder how long you can keep this secret, fearing what will happen if it's revealed. But what if there's hope to be found on the other side? What if it turns out the One you've been hiding from is the One who wants to protect you from the shame?

The Adulterous Woman's Story

Whether prostitution or adultery or some other form, sexual sin exacts a heavy price from women. In it, we sin against our own body (1 Corinthians 6:18). These sins can carry devastating consequences physically and emotionally—especially in communities where sexual sin carries additional social stigma. In the account of Jesus interacting with a woman caught in adultery, however, we see a vivid portrait of him as our Protector, even when we break his law and his heart.

Although this story is not found in all versions of the Bible, many biblical scholars consider the picture we have of Jesus here to be consistent with who he is in other portions of Scripture. I agree. In this passage we see Jesus doing what he often did: afflicting the comfortable and comforting the afflicted. I encourage you to read this story found in John 8:1–11.

As the account begins, it is morning. Jesus has come from the Mount of Olives to the temple to teach. John 8:2 tells us, "All the people came to him," so we know that a huge crowd, representing a cross section of the city's people, has gathered to hear this man about whom the whole city is buzzing.

As for the woman caught in adultery, if she could speak to us today, perhaps this is what she would say:

Before our tryst, I told my lover, "This is the last time. If we are found out, it will be the end of us."

And then, in the middle of our pleasure, we were caught, like a fish on a hook, twisting in horror before the prying eyes of a group of scribes and Pharisees. I was in a living nightmare, the one where you are walking the streets naked for all to see. All they allowed me was a sheet to wrap hurriedly around my body.

I could feel what was coming as my accusers dragged me through street after winding street toward the temple. I heard them hatch their deadly plot between gritted teeth as they forced a path through the teeming streets of Jerusalem: "We've got him now. There's no way he can get away this time."

Him? The man with me escaped without so much as a slap on his hand. Who did they mean?

It didn't take long to discover they were on a mission, and I was simply a pawn in a game they were playing with Jesus of Nazareth.

I had heard of this man, though I had never listened to his teaching. Everyone had an opinion about him, for better or worse. And now he was to be my judge. Wonderful. Another holy man who would dispatch me in short order.

I heard a voice, calm and authoritative, in the distance as we approached the temple. Suddenly, my captors thrust me roughly into the middle of the crowd. Sweating with icy fear and trembling in shame, I was made to stand in front of Jesus.

"Teacher," one of my accusers announced, "this woman has been caught in the act of adultery. Now, in the Law, Moses commanded us to stone such women. So what do you say?"

I shut my eyes against the court before me. How I longed to fall through a hole in the earth, to disappear forever from the blinding sun and glaring eyes and angry voices.

When the Pharisees' question came, I knew my time was at hand. And I saw what they were doing. Jesus would either pronounce judgment on me then, or suggest I be brought to the Romans. Under Roman occupation, Jews were not allowed to pass the death sentence beyond the reach of the Roman judicial system. So if Jesus called for my death, the religious leaders would go to the Roman authorities and tell them he was operating outside their authority. If Jesus said I was not to be stoned, they would run to the Sanhedrin and denounce him as a heretic who did not support the Law of Moses. Either way, they had him.

Either way, I was done for.

Yet all I heard was silence.

Moments later I made out the sound of someone scratching

in the dirt. More angry voices called out, clamoring for an answer.

And then I heard a voice I will never forget: it was unshakable, carrying the wisdom and authority of a thousand judges: "Let him who is without sin among you be the first to throw a stone at her."

Had I heard correctly? What was Jesus of Nazareth saying? Everyone knew these men tithed their mint and cumin; surely, they were blameless by the standards of the Law.

Eyes clenched, I braced myself for the first blow, expecting it to be followed quickly by a crescendo of many more.

Instead, one by one, I heard the sound of stones hitting the road with a *thud . . . thud, thud, thud . . . thud.* Then I discerned the somber retreat of footsteps as my accusers turned and walked away.

When all was quiet, I dared to open my eyes and look at Jesus. To be honest, I had expected a bigger frame, a more winsome face, this man who had captured the attention of Jerusalem.

But his eyes. I have never seen their equal. They were to me a refuge, from which poured a strange mixture of sadness, anger, purity, compassion, and love.

They revealed me as I had never seen myself before. I fell farther short of God's holy law than I had imagined. But I also knew, as never before, just how precious I was. How could that be?

Just minutes before, my heart had cried out, "Oh, God. Oh, God. I can't believe this is happening to me. I want to die. Just let me die. I am completely exposed, and there is no one to protect me."

But now, in the presence of Jesus of Nazareth, my first thought was not horror at being caught. No, my soul was sick with the thought that this truly holy man knew I had slept with a man who was not my husband. It filled me with revulsion and a desire to be clean.

> **But his eyes. I have never seen their equal. They were to me a refuge, from which poured a strange mixture of sadness, anger, purity, compassion, and love.**

My eyes met his again, and in that moment, I knew Jesus had done for me what I could not do for myself. For the first time since I had been taken captive, I took a deep breath and exhaled it fully. I knew I was safe in this man's presence. He had somehow protected me from death. But what about the shame that still clung to me like a suffocating shroud?

Then this holy man stood from where he had been writing on the ground. He looked at me—a guilty woman—full in the face and asked me, "Woman, where are they? Has no one condemned you?"

Awestruck, I glanced around and realized the street was empty except for Jesus, a few of his followers, and me.

"No one, Lord," I managed to stammer.

And then I heard the most beautiful words of my life: "Neither do I condemn you; go, and from now on sin no more." In that moment, I felt shame fall away from me, an unholy mantle I no longer had to conceal myself with.

I walked away a free and different woman.

In the days that followed, when Jesus of Nazareth was himself captured by the same holy men who had caught me, I followed his story closely. The days of his entering Jerusalem during the Feasts of Passover, Firstfruits, and Unleavened Bread. I witnessed his arrest, his trial before the high priests and Pilate himself. I watched as he carried his cross to Golgotha and the soldiers raised his broken body high for all to see.

And when I heard Jesus cry out in agony, "My God, my God, why have you forsaken me?" I knew Jesus was experiencing in far greater measure the sense of shame and abandonment I had felt on the day I met him. Tears pooling in my eyes, the truth burst with clarity before me: Jesus had been condemned to death *in my place*. And I was now free.

Self-Shaming and Self-Effort

The woman caught in adultery came within a hair's breadth of losing her life—and she knew it. She encountered the living God in Jesus Christ. The grace Jesus extended to her changed everything about who she was (loved) and how she lived going forward (free).

The woman's shame became an unforeseen portal into Jesus's sacred refuge. Sister, what if this is also true for you?

In chapter 1, I shared about my early childhood experience with abandonment. After my dad left our family, I hid in the shame of not being "good enough" to hold him within the circle of our family.

Many of us carry our shame-based identities well into adulthood. Maybe like the woman in John 8, we get entangled in an adulterous affair in a vain attempt to feel special and wanted. Maybe we gossip about the new family at church, ignore someone's plea for help, or wallow in self-pity. If we are like most people, the default response to our sin is probably to hide from God in shame and self-hatred. We think, *God's sick and tired of hearing me confess the same old stuff again and again. I'm just going to hide out here for a while and hope he doesn't notice.*

Others of us hide in shame by building our lives as an outer shell of perfection. We try desperately to cover up or compensate for our sins. Until the truth of the gospel penetrated deeply into my spirit, that's how I coped with my shame.

> **TRANSFORMING TRUTH**
>
> Shame sneers, "Your sin is too serious for God to ever pardon." But Christ's forgiveness seeps into your spirit with healing hope that says, "All has been paid for, and your shame removed. You are mine."

The woman caught in adultery clutched desperately at a blanket to cover her nakedness and shame. Are we any different? Not wanting others to notice our failures, we cover ourselves in perfectionism or control. For years I tried to cover up my sins with heroic self-effort. *If I try harder to do all the things on the "Good Christian Woman" job description, God will relent. He won't hold me responsible for all the ways I have blown it.* But striving turned out to be an unsuccessful way of hiding from the truth. It became a means of avoiding repentance by trying to become my own savior.

Can you relate? Are there any other exhausted superwomen out there ready to hang up their capes? God's good gift to me (and all those who come to him) is the sacred refuge that allows me to rest in Jesus. He alone is my Protector because he alone has the power to make me right with God, the Holy One.

Sheltered by Jesus, Our Protector

What the scribes and Pharisees of Jesus's day didn't understand is that the Law will never shelter us because we cannot maintain it. We desperately need someone who can keep the Law *for* us.

Tim Keller said that Jesus's message to us in the gospel is this: "I lived the Sermon on the Mount. . . . Life at its highest. Human life as it ought to be. I did it. And I'm the only one who ever did it. . . . I did it and earned God's blessing, but then I went to the cross and took God's curse. . . . When you believe in me, when you rest in me by faith as your Lord and Savior, then all that you deserve comes on me, and all that I deserve is accredited to you. And now God loves you and accepts you and delights in you as if you did everything I have done."[1]

When our sin explodes with devastating consequences, Jesus protects us with his shelter!

How exactly does this work, you ask, especially when our sin leaves irreparable damage? The apostle Paul explained exactly how Jesus created an unassailable refuge for us. In his letter to the Corinthians, Paul wrote, "For our sake [God] made [Jesus] to be sin who knew no sin, so that in him we might become the righteousness of God" (2 Corinthians 5:21). You see, sister, Jesus's refuge isn't a place to run away *from* sin; it's the place we run *to*, where sin's power to hold us in shame is forever destroyed!

Cosmic Transaction

Picture a cosmic transaction happening before your eyes. Perhaps our sister caught in adultery is here with us as we stand before the cross of Jesus Christ. We are among the women who do not abandon him in his worst hour.

Jesus, the one Paul said "knew no sin," has *become* our sin in the work of atonement. Jesus has become my greed, your gossip, Adam and Eve's rebellion, the woman's adultery. And the Father is punishing that sin with the super-atomic force of his wrath. Being fully holy, the Father cannot look on sin.

So in this moment, the Father looks away from the Son (and our sin). Is it any wonder that Jesus cries out in agony, *"Eli, Eli, lema sabachthani"* ("My God, my God, why have you forsaken me?") in Matthew 27:46? In this moment Jesus Christ is experiencing the Father's utter abandonment. The One who came to shelter us is completely exposed, with no one to help.

But don't miss this if, like me, you often try to save yourself: Jesus endured his Father's rejection so that we will never have to! Shame tries to bully us into believing we're too much of a mess for God. But it turns out that if we bring that mess to Jesus, he's already paid the price to clean it up.

There is no trap door waiting for us as we make our way to the throne of God. The way out of hiding and into the loving presence of the One who forgives us is paved with Jesus's perfect righteousness—not ours. Sister, if your crisis has you hiding in shame, God has provided a way out of your fear of being exposed. And it starts with trusting that Jesus has completely transformed how the Father now sees you.

Jesus Is the Lens

In 2 Corinthians 5:21, Paul added another element to this cosmic exchange. Not only did Christ become our sin, but he also gave us his righteousness. Yes, you read correctly! Are you in Christ? Then Jesus has become the lens through which the Father now sees you—righteous, obedient, delightful, and beloved.

Are you tempted to doubt God's love for you? Doubt no more. At the cross Jesus was exiled from the Father's fellowship so that you can be welcomed home with great joy and complete forgiveness. Let this reality transform how you approach God in your current crisis.

> **Jesus has become the lens through which the Father now sees you—righteous, obedient, delightful, and beloved.**

This reality builds a shelter for you that no one can ever destroy. As Jesus cries out in agony at the Father's rejection of him, as he receives the wrath of the Father meant for us, as he gives us his righteousness, and as he arises a victor over the grave, our mighty Protector builds a shelter for us to live in with him forever.

Even now, can you hear the voice of Jesus, your Protector, calling you out of hiding *from* God and into a place of refuge *with* God? This sacred refuge is a massive tower unassailable by any enemy because it has been built by God himself.

Whether you have lived in bitterness, promiscuity, or adultery, you are a slave to sin that only Jesus can free you from. One sin is not worse than the other. All of us need the power of Christ to change, and Christ can alter the trajectory of our lives because of this "cosmic transaction" that took place on the cross. When you come to Jesus, God does not see your sin any longer. He removes it as far as the east is from the west (Psalm 103:12). He now sees you as righteous because when he looks at you, he sees his Son.

Further, God also sees you as the gifted, called, and unique person he created you to be—the one you can become as the Holy Spirit convicts you of sin and leads you to repentance. Jesus took on the adulteress's sin and saw her innate value. Seeing herself as Jesus saw her inspired her to change, free of any shame. Jesus is offering you the same, sister.

Will the trek out of hiding and into God's refuge in Christ be easy? No, but whether you have been caught in shame or self-effort, this can be the day you come out of hiding. This is your invitation to turn from darkness into the light and shelter of your core identity in Christ. This is the beginning of being transformed from the inside out. Sheltering yourself in the One who frees you from condemnation is the essential first step to finding the abundant life God promises you in Christ. This is the only solution possible for those of us in this sisterhood of suffering and solace. It is the only solution we need.

Enter the Sacred Refuge
of the One Who Forgives You

Jesus may be saying something like this to you:

> Beloved, I see you. Bruised. Broken by sin. I know how deeply old guilt is still engraved in your memory and your heart. It replays in your head on continuous repeat. Those episodes still haunt you and hold you back from receiving your full inheritance as part of my beloved bride. Month by month, year by year, your old sin has sat in your spirit like a festering wound,

telling you, "You can't risk exposure; there's no one to protect you from this."

You've fallen for the lie that my forgiveness is for everybody else, but not you. That I couldn't really forgive the mistakes of your past.

Dear one, because you are mine, your past sin is gone. Paid for. It has been moved as far as the east is from the west. If thoughts of accusation continue to assail you, they are not from me. Take captive every thought and make it obedient to me. Turn your mind to who *I* say you are: blood-bought and righteous. As I became your sin on the cross and experienced the Father's abandonment, I carried the shame of your sin. When I arose a victor over sin and death, I eradicated—once and for all—what put you into shame.

So why are you still hiding from me? As I look at you now, all I see is my righteousness, and you are delightful to me.

How I have missed seeing your face turned toward me. It is time to come out of hiding, dear one. There is a safe place for you in my love and presence.

This sin has cost you so much, beloved. It has isolated you as you have hidden away your face from the Father. It has cut you off from others as you only let them see your false self, telling the world "all is well" when it is not. All along you have been slowly dying inside. And your failures have isolated you even from yourself as self-hatred, victim mentality, or blame-shifting have kept you from doing the hard work of facing your sin with me, fully confessing it, and watching it fall away forever in the sea of forgetfulness. Have you forgotten what it means to live by faith in union with me, to bring your sin to me in full sight of the cross?

I call you to repent—once and for all—and to trust that I was condemned so that you would not be. Beloved, let this be the day when you stop hiding *from* me and begin to hide *in* me. Look in my eyes. Let my arms shelter you now.[2]

REST Under His Wings
Spend time quieting yourself in God's presence.

Release your sin.
1. What secrets do you keep? What past (or present) sin still lurks in the back corner of your mind—haunting you with its graphic details?
2. How much mileage has the enemy gotten out of these sins still chaining you to the past? What kind of sorrow or pain have they caused?
3. How has hiding from God in shame affected your relationship with Jesus? Write a prayer to the Lord, pouring out your heart to him about this.

Father, I come to you now, recognizing that I have unconfessed sin I have been afraid to bring to you. You know it all, Father. But now in the sacred shelter of Jesus, I confess and release the sins of _____.

Exchange your *shame* for the shelter of Jesus's *forgiveness.*
4. Have you been turning to self-effort to avoid feelings of shame? If so, what impact have those efforts had on you? What would be different for you if you received Jesus's forgiveness instead?

Father, you know I have hidden in shame, and it has cost me so much. I am done running and pretending. I give you my shame and receive your full and free pardon. I trust that I am now covered and protected. By faith, I enter the sacred refuge you have built for me in Jesus's righteousness.

See yourself in union with Christ.

5. What truths will you turn to if you feel shame coming back to haunt you? Ask God to help you live in light of your union with Christ.

Father, when the accuser comes to bother me, help me to take captive every thought and make it obedient to Christ as I remember who I am in him.

Trust Christ as the one who shelters you in his righteousness.

6. Create a breath prayer, a simple response to the Lord. (For example: "Jesus . . . thank you for taking my sin." Or "Lord . . . I release my shame." Or "Father . . . I come clean into your presence.") Use this prayer as a reminder to trust in Jesus's forgiveness throughout your day.

PART TWO

Abiding in Sacred Refuge

SISTER, YOU'VE MADE good progress in discovering God's safe place for you. But as comforting as it is to *find* sacred refuge, God has far more for you. He wants to help you *abide* in this wonderful shelter with him. There's a difference between visiting God's refuge and making it your home.

Consider this an official invitation to a permanent change of address. It's time to discover how to actually *dwell* in God's refuge, tucked up under his wings in the shadow of the Almighty (Psalm 91:1), safe from whatever life throws at you.

This is what our sacred sisters will teach us in this part of *Sacred Refuge.* They struggled with a variety of crises that caused them to cry out: "Can God restore my health and peace?" "Can I really trust God to meet my needs?" "Can God give someone with my past a new beginning?" "Can I still come home, even when I've wandered from God?"

"When my heart is broken in disappointment, can I still trust God?" As we'll see, God's resounding answer is "Yes!"—if we're willing to abide in the sacred refuge he has built for us.

God is inviting you to make that hiding place under his wings your heart's true home. Lean in and listen closely, sister. You may hear the Lord saying, "Come up under here, my beloved one. There is a place reserved for you next to my heart. Come abide with me."

CHAPTER 4

Healed

Finding Shelter in the Great Physician

He will cover you with his pinions,
and under his wings you will find refuge;
his faithfulness is a shield and buckler.
—Psalm 91:4

Can God restore my
health and peace?

ON THE PHONE, a friend shared about a serious problem she and her family were navigating. I listened as she unburdened what she was carrying. We discussed the reality that God was able to bring good from the situation and even use it to teach her and others more about who he is.

"Never waste a good crisis," I offered, just a little too glibly.

A few hours later, I got a call from my doctor's office.

"Ms. Rienstra, the results of your recent mammogram show some abnormalities. The radiologist would like to take a second look. Are you able to come back to the diagnostic center for another mammogram—perhaps later this week?"

My heart dropped in my chest. "Uh, yes," I stammered. "I can do that."

That "second look" turned into an ultrasound, which, a week later, turned into a biopsy.

After the procedure, I processed the films with the radiologist, who pointed to a dark circle in my left breast. "I'm seeing a mass with some irregularities," she said in a too-calm voice. "That is concerning, but we will send these biopsy samples to the lab and see what comes back."

Right, I thought to myself. Translation: "Buckle your seat belt; this ride might get a little bumpy." Two days later, I got the call.

"Ms. Rienstra, the lab results show you have an infiltrating mammary carcinoma. Cancer."

There it was. The C-word. Used in the same sentence as my name. The world tilted a little bit, and I fought the sensation that this surreal scenario was happening to someone else. Not me.

Thus began weeks of blood draws, appointments with an oncologist, surgeon, even genetic specialists. I heard, "We need to be sure you don't have the BRCA1 gene; if so, you are probably looking at a mastectomy."

My imagination began to conjure scary pictures of my body mutilated from radical surgery. God intervened through a friend who reminded me of Elisabeth Elliot's wise words: "There is no grace for the imagination."[1] Indeed.

And yet, in the midst of all the scary scenarios playing out in my mind, grace is what I longed for most. The grace of physical healing, of course. But what I needed even more for my journey was the grace of a heart healed of its worry and doubts.

The Journey No One Wants to Take

Sister, I know some of you are walking this road, or a similar one, right now. You are traveling through your own health crisis. You got the phone call with news you didn't want to hear. You are dealing with chronic pain or the side effects of treatment. Your car has traveled too many miles between hospitals and doctors' offices. You've been wading through the swamp of medications, treatments, and side effects—a journey you never signed up for.

Or perhaps you're supporting a loved one through their health crisis. You find yourself lost in the morass of appointments, bills, and medications—not to mention the worry you carry for their future. Will they be healed? Will all return to normal?

You want to pray and hope for healing, but you know God doesn't choose to heal everyone. Worry—about the future, mounting medical bills, pain management—is gnawing away at your peace.

Maybe what you are walking through is compounded by the belief—as many in Jesus's day thought—that your sickness is the direct result of your sin. "God is paying you back for all your mistakes," whispers the enemy of your soul. Lately, when the fear creeps quietly into your mind at night, you've begun to wonder if he's right.

Your heart may be crying, *Can God really heal me and restore my peace?*

This year my own health crisis solidified my confidence in this truth: There is a Great Physician who is watching over your case with exacting care and gentleness. Nothing misses his gaze or attention. His hand is able to reach you—your heart, your body, your situation. He may be saying to you right now: *Dear one, I am here. There is refuge available to you right now in me. I am Jesus, your Healer. Come, let me hold you in the safety of my embrace.*

The Bleeding Woman's Story

Scripture provides us with stories of many sacred sisters who longed for God's healing embrace. Women who struggled with infertility, yearning for children to hold in their arms. Mothers begging for merciful healing on behalf of their children. Women wrestling with physical ailments that wracked their broken bodies with pain.

We read of one such woman who sought out Jesus in the middle of a busy crowd, desperate to be rid of her disease. She hadn't meant to cause a commotion. Attention was the last thing she wanted. But when the woman with an issue of blood heard that Jesus of Nazareth had returned to Galilee, she knew she had to see him.

The gospel writers tell us that this woman suffered from a bleeding disorder for more than a decade. And while we don't know for certain what her disease was, we do know that it isolated her from community. Based on the requirements of the Jewish law in those days, bleeding was a condition that made people unclean—as well as anyone who touched them (Leviticus 15:25). When a woman's bleeding ended, she could go through ritual purification to be considered clean and engage with others once again. But what about a woman who never stopped bleeding?

This was the dilemma of the woman with an issue of blood. And her condition likely meant not only physical pain but the emotional pain of isolation as well. You can read about her in the gospel accounts in Matthew 9:20–23 and Mark 5:25–34, but please read Luke 8:40–56, where we will focus our attention. I imagine this is how our dear sister might have told her story:

It had been twelve years. Four thousand three hundred and eighty days, to be exact. I watched most of my children grow into adulthood since the time the bleeding began. Twelve years of trying to staunch a flow of blood that would not stop and living with the embarrassing telltale signs. My body had betrayed me, and I was caught in a living death. I was unseen, unclean, unwanted.

"It will pass after a few months," one healer had assured me, his palm outstretched to collect the fee for his services.

Another so-called healer suggested I wear a special amulet to ward off evil spirits, as it was clear to him I was cursed. Lucky me: he was running a special price on amulets that day.

As months of bleeding turned into years, my husband grew impatient. For the unceasing flow of blood not only left me exhausted; it also made me ceremonially unclean. That meant no marital relations.

It also meant that when I went into public, to the market, people scurried away from me. Vendors stopped doing business with me, certain I would contaminate them. I was no longer able to attend worship at my synagogue; how I missed being with God's people in his house!

The worst part of the bleeding was isolation. Forced to hide myself away, I became increasingly depressed and desperate to find a path back to life.

So I followed every lead, tracked down every possible healer, swallowed every noxious potion I was offered. No one could do a thing for me. With each attempt, my hope died another small death, my savings shrank, and my condition worsened. I still remember the day I looked in my small leather purse and found it empty. I had exhausted every possibility, spent every denarius. And still my bleeding continued.

"Hopeless," said the last healer I consulted. "Your case is hopeless. This condition will be the end of you." His words sounded like the clanging of prison doors, shutting me inside a dark place from which hope had fled.

Then one day I heard that Jesus of Nazareth had returned to Galilee. A sliver of hope broke into my prison cell. It was said that with one touch he was able to give sight to the blind and restore lepers to full health. *One touch.*

I had not been touched in over a decade. Could such a man help someone like me?

I was only one of the many who flocked to see Jesus that day. Desperate enough to brave the crowds that followed him, I reasoned, *No one here would let me close to them if they knew of my uncleanness. If someone recognizes me as the bleeding woman, they might call me out. I will have to retreat, and I will lose my one last chance at healing.*

Coming up from behind, I saw the Savior. He was standing in the eye of a roiling storm of people shouting for his attention. I was surprised to see Jairus, a leader from my local synagogue, among them. This prominent man was kneeling before Jesus, asking him to come heal his little daughter, who was close to dying. When Jesus began to move again, and the crowd closed in to follow him, I saw my opportunity and fought my way through.

As Jesus headed toward Jairus's house, I crouched down

behind him, out of his sight. No one would know I had touched the Teacher. This was my last chance, and I knew it.

Simply a touch of his garment would do. But just as I reached out toward Jesus, someone in the crowd jostled me. All I could grasp was the hem of his robe.

But it was enough!

Immediately, I experienced a warm, healing power radiate throughout my body. And the flow of blood stopped.

All I could grasp was the hem of his robe. But it was enough!

However, my elation quickly became panic when Jesus asked, "Who was it that touched me?" No one replied. Then one of his followers stated the obvious: "Master, the crowds surround you and are pressing in on you!"

But Jesus persisted, "Someone touched me, for I perceive that power has gone out from me."

He had been on his way to the house of an important leader in our synagogue. Who was I to draw his attention? All I had known for twelve years was a life in the margins. Part of me had grown used to being unseen, unknown, and unloved. Hiding in the shadows had become my unwelcome home. At that moment, I longed to slip away.

Uninvited, I had taken something from him. How I needed his mercy!

I knew my body was healed. But so did the One who had made it possible. Trembling, I fell down before Jesus and began to speak.

The crowd pulled back, surprised by my presence and

afraid of becoming unclean themselves. At the same time, they knew they were witnessing a miracle. Their babble fell to a hush as I continued.

The words poured out of me just as the blood had—a hot flow of emotion and suffering and helplessness.

Finally, I added, "And so, Master, this is why I touched you just now. Desperation drove me to it. But how thankful I am, Teacher. How grateful. Because as soon as I touched the fringe of your garment, I . . . I was healed."

The crowd gasped. "Healed by his touch." "Did you hear that?" "One touch was all it took to heal this poor woman."

I thought Jesus would chastise me for touching him. Instead, he looked at me with unexpected compassion. In his eyes I saw an invitation to come out of the shadows and step into the open where he stood.

But he wasn't finished. He gave me far more than I had hoped for. More than just physical healing, Jesus created a permanent refuge for me to live in from that day on.

In that moment, it was as if the crowd didn't exist. It was just Jesus and me, eyes locked. Then he spoke directly to me, his words flowing like healing balm.

"Daughter, your faith has made you well; go in peace."

Had Jesus really called me "daughter"? He had. With one word he removed my "unclean" status and invited me into the full rights of the family of faith. He lifted me from life in the gutter and restored me to my community in Galilee.

In doing so, and without physical touch, Jesus's words reached a deep place of emotional palsy in my spirit. It had been shut up long ago, infected by worry, self-hatred, and loneliness. As Jesus spoke, the doors burst open, and light and hope flooded in.

Then the Teacher said to me, "Go in shalom." It was a simple but powerful blessing, and my spirit drank it in like a desert traveler stumbling upon fresh springs. Jesus's words echoed in my mind until the end of my days: "Be filled with peace, daughter of God. Go forth and live from a place of wholeness and well-being."

The woman's physical wounds were healed by the One who had designed and made her. More than that, her spiritual and emotional wounds were healed by the One who would be wounded on her behalf. The Great Physician would bleed so she could be whole. And by his wounds, she would be fully healed (Isaiah 53:5).

UNDER HIS WINGS

In the Law given through Moses in Numbers 15:38–39, God instructed his people to "make tassels on the corners of their garments throughout their generations . . . [to] remember all the commandments of the Lord." Interestingly, the word used for the corners of Jewish religious robes is the same word used for "wings" in many Old Testament passages, such as Malachi 4:2—a prophecy saying the coming Messiah "shall rise with healing in [his] wings."

In this story of Jesus healing the bleeding woman, we witness a beautiful picture of this prophecy in action. Messiah would come with healing in his "wings"—remember, also the word for the corner of his robe, right where the bleeding woman touched him. Her reaching out to Jesus certainly proved her faith that he could heal her bleeding. More than that, it might have indicated her belief that he was the Messiah, come to secure her ultimate healing.

Longing for Normal

Sister, what physical or mental illness are you (or a loved one) fighting? Has it isolated you? Do you sense a shift in how others perceive and treat you? I discovered through my cancer diagnosis that sickness often sets us apart from normal social interaction. People don't seem to know what to say to you, except to ask about your sickness. Your regular, true self feels unseen. Maybe you used to help others in your community, but now you feel relegated to the "needs help" category.

As you navigate this health crisis, what lies have you been tempted to believe? Has the thought invaded that you are somehow being punished for past sins through this illness? How are you refuting this pernicious deception from the enemy?

Sickness has a way of bringing us to the end of ourselves—the place we spend most of our lives trying to avoid. The difference between the word *scared* and the word *sacred* is just the transposition of two letters. But what a world of difference in meaning! Seeing our limitations *is* painful and scary. But what if this is the very place God is tenderly leading you—to reveal more of his holiness and power made manifest in your weakness? What if he's inviting you to encounter him in your sickness as you never have before?

When we are ill, the uncertainty of outcomes can do a number on our relationship with God. It can tempt us down a path of pain and worry that leads us away from his comfort and truth. It can lead us into hiding from the very source of our healing and help. So how do we cross the threshold from hiding and into God's sacred refuge?

Sheltered by Jesus, Our Healer

During the process of discovering that cancer was in my body and following medical protocols to eradicate this foreign invader, I came face-to-face with my mortality. Perhaps you have also been there—or are walking this strange path right now. I wrestled with the possibility that this disease might take me out . . . as it had three friends over the last four years.

But just when I was most overwhelmed, God reminded me of the powerful promise from the prophet Malachi. Even as God warned his people about judgment to come in the last days, he offered this picture of how Jesus would bring healing to his people: "But to you who fear

My name the Sun of Righteousness shall arise with healing in His wings" (Malachi 4:2 NKJV).

Did you catch it? The *Sun* of Righteousness foreshadows the *Son* of Righteousness, and God's promise is that he, Jesus Christ, will bring healing as he rises from the grave.

Experts agree that "the 'Sun of Righteousness' is an unmistakable reference to the Messiah, Jesus Christ, the Light of the World."[2]

We see the wing metaphor used as Jesus looked over Jerusalem, his heart aching. "O Jerusalem, Jerusalem, the city that kills the prophets and stones those who are sent to it! How often would I have gathered your children together as a hen gathers her brood under her wings, and you were not willing!" (Matthew 23:37).

> **TRANSFORMING TRUTH**
>
> Isolation says, "You are alone, and you will always be alone." But the voice of Jesus says, "I am here, beloved. As your Great Physician, I am with you right now to bring you wholeness and peace."

These images of Jesus rising in triumphant flight—with healing in his very "wings"—or as a mother gathering her chicks to protect them are fascinating pictures that align with the image God gives us in Psalm 91:1–4 expressing his desire to shelter us under his wings:

> He who dwells in the shelter of the Most High
> will abide in the shadow of the Almighty.
> I will say to the LORD, "My refuge and my fortress,
> my God, in whom I trust."
> For he will deliver you from the snare of the fowler
> and from the deadly pestilence.
> He will cover you with his pinions,
> and under his wings you will find refuge.

A Shelter from Fear

Notice that God gives this truth about his wings of refuge to us in the form of an invitation. It's as though he's beckoning to us with these verses and saying, "Do you long to get out of the scorching heat of life? Do you long for cooling shade and rest in my presence? Does your soul need healing? Is your world in chaos? Come under my wings, which I spread out in love for you on the cross. I am your refuge."

Sister, Jesus is our sacred "refuge and fortress" (v. 2). He is the God in whom we can fully trust. More than that, he has already delivered us from the "fowler's snare"—the enemy's control. And he's saved us from the "deadly pestilence"—the effect of sin, which is death.

> ## "Come under my wings, which I spread out in love for you on the cross. I am your refuge."

Jesus is the compassionate one who longs to cover us with "his pinions" (the outer feathers of a bird's wing that allow it to take flight and shelter its babies from harm). But we must come near enough for him to do that. As we nestle in under his wings, we will find refuge (v. 4). As we turn to him amid the pain, we find protection from the worries and doubts that drive us into hiding. We find companionship on the path that can so often be lonely and misunderstood.

None would argue the assertion that cancer is a "deadly pestilence" (v. 3). Statistics now tell us that one in eight women will be diagnosed with breast cancer.[3] Not to mention the other types of cancer we contend with, as well as other types of disease. And many survive. Innovations abound. But it's also no secret that often the best of the medical community's treatment plans is brutal.

Pestilence. Not a bad word to describe it.

In dying my death for me, Jesus has removed my fear of death—by the pestilence of cancer or any other means. The worst thing that can happen to me is that my physical body would cease to function and

I would go immediately into the presence of God as his much-loved child (2 Corinthians 5:8).

If that's the *worst* thing that can happen to me—to be ushered into God's presence—what is there to fear? Everything else—all that cancer might put me through—is covered too, if I experience it all from my position within the sheltering, healing wings of Jesus. How about you? Is your soul confident of the same?

God's invitation to "dwell in the shelter of the Most High" is proof positive that we are not alone in a medical crisis, or any crisis. When you experience the part of your medical journey where even those closest to you cannot travel (being wheeled into surgery, undergoing chemo or excruciating physical therapy), there is One inviting you to find your refuge in him. Ideally, we are already abiding deeply in God. The goal then is to "shelter in place" right in the middle of your crisis. Jesus is there for those who will lean in under his strong, sheltering pinions.

A Shelter to Dwell In

As I moved through surgery and radiation, I knew it was an exceptional blessing to have a caring husband, supportive family, and solid friends. I had thought I understood the reality of God's sheltering love, that Jesus is my refuge.

But that understanding deepened in unforeseen ways. God has invited me to lean in closer to him, to burrow more deeply under his wings. In that place he has filled me supernaturally with his peace. Filled? More than that—*enveloped* me in it.

The day I heard cancer had gained a foothold in my body, I knew my world was about to change. But God sheltered me from panic or wrenching fear just as clearly as if he was standing guard to prevent it from getting near me. As I endured one medical appointment, test, and procedure after another, I sensed God carrying me through each step. As I headed into surgery, he sheltered me in a cocoon of his perfect peace.

Wouldn't that alone have made a sweet testimony to share with friends and family? An encouragement for others facing their own cancer journey? But more of the unexpected lay ahead.

Propped in the passenger seat with my surgical site protected by bandages and a pillow to protect it from the seatbelt strap, I leaned my head against the headrest, grateful for my husband's tender care as we headed home from surgery. I was ready for healing to begin. It had been a rough day physically, but the sun shining on the trees revealed their resplendent beauty. They were a reminder that I was alive and—with the cancer now removed—healing could begin.

Moments later, I was staring down at a lapful of windshield glass, my anesthesia-fogged brain trying to understand why our car was bent so curiously, crippled in the bottom of a ditch. White powder filled the car, now totaled, evidence that the airbags had deployed.

A car at an intersection had run a stop sign and rammed into our car, just in front of where I was sitting. Had we been going a little faster, I would have been T-boned directly. At the moment of impact, with a strange calmness, I remember thinking, *Oh, we've been hit. Oh, Rob's fighting to keep our car from flipping.* Then I sensed the Holy Spirit say, *All will be well.*

I'm not a medical expert, but even I knew that kind of jostling and jolt of adrenaline so soon after surgery couldn't be good . . . for my stitches, for my blood pressure, for the healing I was so desperate to begin.

But even then, at that moment and its aftermath, I felt completely and unexpectedly protected by God's sheltering presence. I was fully protected in sacred refuge.

I was experiencing the same peace (*shalom*) Jesus granted the woman with an issue of blood. It was a peace that surpassed understanding, guarding my heart and mind in Christ Jesus (Philippians 4:7) And it is available to you, my sister.

Since the cancer surgery, car accident, and radiation treatments, I am learning to "*dwell* in the shelter of the Most High," not just reach out for it and give it a loving pat, grateful that it's there if I need it. Rather, I live in it and navigate all of life from inside it. Where I once might have thought his refuge was like a concrete bunker to run to if things got rough, I now know it is a permanent home . . . on wheels. I travel inside it, abide in it, and view life from within it.

God is "my refuge and my fortress, my God in whom I trust." Sacred refuge. Not a refugee camp, but a refuge and home. God protects me here from attacks and snares. And as I nestle into God's presence, tucked under his wings, he covers me with his pinions (Psalm 91:4). Here nothing can touch me or destroy me.

Within this sacred space, when I am very still, I can hear his heartbeat telling me, "I love you. I love you. I love you." Sister, can you hear him singing the same words over you? He promises to do this for his people: "The LORD your God is in your midst, a mighty one who will save; he will rejoice over you with gladness; he will quiet you by his love; he will exult over you with loud singing" (Zephaniah 3:17).

Sheltered Under His Wings

Something extraordinary has been happening to me over the last few months that echoes this theme of birds nestling under a parental wing. Every few days, perhaps two or three times a week, I find a feather. It might be on the side of the road as I am walking in my neighborhood. It could be a tiny down feather I find in a completely random place in my house or in a store. Last week, on a one-day trip to Atlanta, I found eight of them. Yesterday, it was an iridescent two-inch-long bluebird feather. I have collected them in a china bowl, not sure what to make of them.

After telling a friend about the collection, she said God had also put feathers in her path several years ago (who would have guessed?). She reminded me of the Psalm 91 passage. Sometimes I am stunned by how creatively God speaks to us!

Another friend's heart was broken by unwanted and unexpected divorce. For years afterward, she could barely walk a path or stroll the beach without finding a heart-shaped rock, as if God knew she needed a reminder that he cared, he saw her, she was not forgotten, and her heart's healing was found in her Creator's embrace.

Throughout my recent illness, God has dropped feathers in my path as a visual reminder of his presence and promise to shelter me. He invites me to nestle into his sacred refuge, deeper into his heart and protection. Whatever the next steps or the eventual outcome, he invites me "further up and further in" to the shelter only he can give.[4]

I don't know the nature of the pestilence that's stalking you right now. But I do know how physical sickness can so easily morph into heartsickness. Fears. Doubts about God's care. Isolation. These can afflict our spirits as brutally as disease afflicts our bodies. But what if it's precisely in the midst of all this pain that Jesus wants to give you the miracle of his refuge?

When fear begins to creep into my own journey, I hear God's invitation: "Come deeper into the shelter, beloved one. I am here to cover you under my wings." These are the wings of the infinite One. There's room for you here too. Won't you come nestle under his sheltering love?

Enter the Sacred Refuge of Jesus, Your Healer

Jesus may be saying something like this to you:

> Beloved, I know you long to be healed, to have peace restored to your life. I see your pain. I know you are afraid. You wonder, *Did this happen because of my sin? Where will this lead? Will I survive this? Will I have to endure much pain?* As these thoughts and fears roll through your mind, again and again, your anxiety begins to rise.
>
> But this is not your inheritance, beloved. I offer you another way, a way of peace. It is found in remembering whose you are.
>
> The Father put you into me, did he not? Your life is now

hidden in mine. That means that nothing can reach you apart from the will of the Father to bring good out of it—for you and for others.

Can you trust that even now I am sheltering you in this hard season? For I am your safe place to run to when your imagination takes you to dark places. And when fear comes knocking, ask me to answer the door. Then fear will surely flee!

It's time to come out of the storm, beloved. I invite you now to experience me as your shelter. Turn away from the confusion, the lies, the what-ifs, and step toward me instead. That's it. Look up and remember who I am; worship and remind yourself of my strength, majesty, power, and loving-kindness.

Enter into my presence; cross over the threshold and come all the way into the shelter of my arms. Now abide deeply in my love for you; it is your place of safety and rest. As you lay your head upon my breast, you will hear my heart beating in love for you. Let this comfort and calm you as it does a small bird or tiny child.

Finally, understand that you can navigate this sickness—indeed your whole life—from this safe place in me. You can come as often as you like, not just in the morning, but throughout the day, just to be with me. Come abide in my sheltering love. I long for your presence, beloved. You give me joy.

As you move through this season, know three things:

You are being held (Deuteronomy 33:27; Isaiah 41:13). I am holding on to you, even your very hand, and I will not let go.
You are being heard (Proverbs 15:29; Jeremiah 29:11–13). I have heard your heart cries, and I am at work on your behalf.

You are being healed (Jeremiah 17:14; Psalm 41:3). I have already healed your sin sickness, and I am strengthening you in your inner person.

Remember that I have been where you are. I prayed, and bled, and pleaded with my Father to let the cup of suffering pass from my lips. How I dreaded what I knew was coming! But my deepest longing was for my Father's plan to be fulfilled. And so my prayer became "your will be done." Will you follow in my footsteps in this, beloved? Will you trust that if the Father is allowing this crisis, it is only because great good will come from it?

For by my stripes you are healed, beloved. That may mean that sickness will be removed from your body. It surely means that my suffering on the cross has healed your relationship with the Father—forever.

I am so near to you, beloved, even now. Will you reach out to touch the hem of my garment? Healing and peace await you here under the shelter of my wings.[5]

REST Under His Wings

Spend time quieting yourself in God's presence.

Release control.
1. What physical or mental illness are you fighting? How has it stolen your peace?
2. In your sickness, what lies have you been tempted to believe? (About God? Yourself? The future?)
3. In what ways have you tried to control the outcome of your illness?

Father, I come to you now, recognizing that I am not in control. I do not know the way ahead. But you do. I now relinquish control and put myself completely in your hands.

Exchange your *sickness* and *isolation* for the shelter of Christ's *healing peace*.

4. How have your worries or isolation affected your relationship with Jesus?

5. Write a prayer describing your needs and giving each one to Jesus, your Healer.

Father, I have hidden from you in this sickness, thinking this was the result of my sin. I see now that this is a lie. Please forgive me and draw me into your sacred refuge.

See yourself in union with Christ.

6. What is one practice that might help you seek Jesus's presence amid your current struggle? What could you try when worry or isolation start to batter your heart?

Father, my life is yours, not mine. You know I struggle with fear of the future, but right now I ask you to help me cross the threshold out of hiding and into your beautiful and sacred refuge in Jesus.

Trust Christ as the one who shelters you in his healing power.

7. Create a breath prayer that expresses your trust in the Lord. (For example: "Jesus . . . please heal me." Or "Jehovah . . . you are my healer." Or "I am being held. . . . I am being heard. . . . I am being healed.") Pray this breath prayer often as you continue to walk out of hiding and into God's sheltering presence.

CHAPTER 5

Provided For

Finding Shelter in the God of All Supply

But let all who take refuge in you rejoice;
let them ever sing for joy,
and spread your protection over them,
that those who love your name may exult in you.
—PSALM 5:11

Can I really trust God to meet my needs?

ONE HUNDRED SIXTY-FIVE dollars and twenty-six cents. This was the grand total of the bank account my husband and I shared three years into our marriage.

It was early September. Rob and I had just returned from a summer-long trip to South Korea where we had served short-term with Mission to the World. God had provided funds for us to go through the generosity of our church in New Jersey. It had been a wondrous time of teaching English to Koreans heading out as missionaries to many countries across the globe. They, in turn, taught us how to pray.

Now the summer was over, and I was one week out from resuming my job teaching high school English. The next day Rob would return for his third year of seminary. Or not.

To start classes, he first had to pay what was, for us, a massive bill at the bursar's office.

A lot was riding on paying that bill, including Rob's ability to pursue his calling of becoming a pastor. We checked the amount in our bank account again. We rechecked the amount of his bill. Deflated, we knew we were in over our heads. A sick uneasiness crept into our stomachs.

"Well, let's pray," Rob initiated. We did. Simply and emphatically, we laid out our need to the God who had called us to go to Korea *and* pursue seminary training. Desperate, we cried out to him and left the matter in his hands.

Half an hour later, we heard a knock at our door. It was a good friend from church. Then single, this friend held a lucrative job as a medical technologist.

"I know this seems strange," she blurted out after we invited her in. "Me just showing up here close to bedtime, unannounced. But I had to come. I was doing my finances tonight, and as I wrote out my checks, God impressed deeply on me that I was to give you what was left in one of my accounts."

She held out a check. "So here it is."

Rob and I just looked at each other. Was this really happening?

"I don't know what it's for, but I trust God does."

Rob took the check and gazed at it, his face unreadable. Then he handed it to me.

I fell back into my chair. It was exactly, to the dollar, the amount we owed the next day for Rob to continue his seminary training.

What a joy it was to tell our friend of our need and let her know that God had met it through her!

Plenty of people have experienced that sick feeling Rob and I had when we knew the bill we owed exceeded our means. Maybe you are there right now.

I hope you have also experienced the provision of God, just as we did for that seminary bill and for the huge college costs we doled out later. As our children approached college and we peered into our miniscule college savings fund, we sensed the Lord say, *What is needed will be provided when it is needed.* He kept that promise over the next seven years, providing one job after another for me, each more demanding and better paying. Each job allowed us to cover double the costs as two children attended college at the same time. And every bill was paid on time!

All too often, however, it feels like the debts pile up faster than we can fill our bank accounts. Ramsey Solutions reports that "the total personal debt in the U.S. is at an all-time high of $17.5 trillion. The average American debt (per U.S. adult) is $66,772, and 77% of American households have at least some type of debt."[1] Some of us live as slaves to these debts and bills, constantly juggling and wondering, *Which bill should I pay this month?*

In an increasingly unjust culture, we may be in debt through no fault of our own. God may allow us to be in financial straits through others' greed or injustice. Unexpected crises may drain our finances. Or our economic distress may be due to unwise decisions that seemed to make sense at the time. Financial struggles can easily lead to identity struggles. Growing up in a single-mom household, I remember the sense of shame attached to using food stamps and receiving government food staples.

In time, we can begin to feel like our identities are tied to our financial situations. Our cultural norm of "I am what I own" becomes "I am what I owe." The crisis of debt turns into desperation, which descends on us like a lead straitjacket that prohibits our freedom and joy.

Have you begun to fall for the lie "I am what I owe"? If so, you are not alone.

A DIFFERENT KIND OF DEBT

We used to call it "keeping up with the Joneses." Our culture's focus on material wealth and collecting more "stuff" pits us against our neighbors so that we feel like losers if we don't have what they have. But social climbing through conspicuous consumption leads to its own kind of debt because it never ends. There's always a new fashion trend to follow. A hot new vacation spot we have to try. A new home decor idea splashed across Pinterest that calls our name. Trying to find our worth and identity in these ways sets off an endless cycle we never reach the end of. It causes a new kind of debt we can never pay off.

The root issue? Believing our culture's lie, expressed in every TV commercial and billboard, that "I am what I own." This fallacy makes fools of those of us in desperate pursuit of the picture-perfect house, chicest outfit, or most prestigious private school for our children. But it also deceives those who may be "hiding" in their money. They might not be mired in debt, but they are looking for identity and security apart from God—perhaps in their own efforts to create wealth. Satan is equally willing to tempt people in this way as well.

Either way, he is hell-bent on keeping us from trusting in God as *Jehovah Jireh,* our Provider God.

Longing for Financial Security

What's your story? Have you lost your husband and are now financially or relationally vulnerable? Perhaps you feel like your family is under attack, just one step away from falling apart. Or maybe your life once felt full, but now all you see are doors closing, opportunities shutting down, and a once-bright future growing smaller and more elusive.

You wake up early in the morning afraid for your children or grandchildren, afraid of running out of money for retirement, afraid of what demands you will face today that you cannot begin to meet alone. When times get especially tight, you wonder, *Can God really provide for me, paying a debt I can never pay?*

Even now, Jesus may be saying to you, "I see you, child. I know your needs. You are free to ask me for provision that only I can make. I will care for you, dear one. Trust me and ask."

What kind of refuge would not also provide for our basic needs? Would Jesus really offer: "Here, you'll be safe in these walls. There's nothing to eat or drink, nothing to keep you warm, nothing with which you can rebuild your strength. But aren't these lovely stone walls?"

That's not what God's refuge is like. In it, we find more than adequate, and often surprisingly abundant, provision. And safe within God's arms, we find an identity that has nothing to do with the size of our bank accounts or the perks we can (or can't) afford. It's the place where God's children are cared for, known, and loved.

Whatever our story, we see a compelling portrait of this shelter in the Old Testament story of a widow who was about to lose everything when God intervened in a miraculous way and revealed himself as her powerful Provider. Her story answers the question many of us ask: "Can God really meet my needs?"

The Widow's Story

We meet this woman at a low ebb in Israel's history. The ten northern tribes of Israel who broke away after Solomon's death had abandoned Jehovah. Incited to rebellion against their God under the leadership of evil King Ahab and nefarious Queen Jezebel, the people were in full-blown apostasy and chaos. They were living immorally, sacrificing their children, and attempting to divine the future from Baal-zebub, the false god of Ekron.

A holy God should have wiped them out.

Instead, he was moving powerfully through his prophets Elijah and then Elisha to call Israel to repentance—to restoration. He longed for their return and faithful adherence to his ways, for then they would enjoy not only closeness to him but all the blessings that flow from obedience.

God was also getting their attention through events in nature. In this season of Israel's abandonment of Jehovah as their ruler, Scripture recounts that "the water is bad, and the land is unfruitful" (2 Kings 2:19). Set during a time when resources were scarce, the widow's story is found in 2 Kings 4:1–7.

If we could hear this sister tell her story, it might sound like this:

Jehovah had warned us back in Moses's day. Follow other gods, reap cursing. No rain for years. Famine in the land.

By the time our two sons were almost grown, food was in such short supply that we ate one meal a day, if we were lucky.

In the middle of Israel's abandonment of Jehovah, God raised up a school of prophets to speak the truth, perform miracles, and point the people back to their true home in him.

These "sons of the prophets" were a God-fearing band who still trusted in Jehovah. My husband, God rest his soul, was one of them.

I remember the day my Lemuel came home and told me how Elijah had parted the waters of the Jordan River and how Elisha purified the waters of Jericho. With every telling of these stories, our family's faith grew. Surely, Jehovah was the one true God—and there was no other!

I would need this strong faith in the days to come because one day, my husband dropped dead on his way back from the city gate.

I had watched other women lose their husbands, seen them age before their time. Often, they moved in with family and lost a home of their own. I observed their descent into obscurity, living out the remainder of their days on the fringes of society—unseen, unheard, unvalued.

Loneliness gnawed at my heart on those first long nights without my husband's comforting presence beside me, those first days of sitting across from the yawning emptiness of his chair at the table. Memories haunted me of better days before famine when we would feast with our boys on simple food and conversation about the goodness of Jehovah.

But I hadn't seen this coming: the empty coffers that mocked me and fueled my growing anxiety about financial ruin. Although my husband had been rich toward God, serving Jehovah faithfully as one of his prophets, he had been less than a great money manager. Neither of us had planned for famine and the destruction of our livelihoods. When Lemuel died unexpectedly, he left my sons and me on the brink of ruin.

And it wasn't that we were overdrawn by a few denarii at our local savings and loan. Or that we still owed last month's bill at the butcher's. No, this debt loomed before me like a mountain I had no means of scaling, casting a long shadow of fear and lack across each day of my grief.

I remember the day I began to panic. A merciless creditor came looking for his due, but this was a debt I could not begin to pay. He sniffed, unaffected. If I did not pay up by a certain date, he would take my two sons as his slaves to work off the unpaid debt. My boys would go from being the free sons of God-fearing parents to slaves at the mercy of a harsh taskmaster. Having lost my dear Lemuel, I now tottered on the verge of an even greater disaster: losing my precious sons and, with them, any sense of future security.

I began to hide out in my house. I didn't want my neighbors to know what was going on. I cried out to God. Hadn't he made several provisions in his law to keep his people out of debt and protect them from this kind of predicament? But I had no nearest relative to stand up and provide for me and my sons as their kinsman-redeemer. There was no extra grain to be gleaned in the fields. My neighbors had deviated from obeying these very laws which might have protected me. And in famine, it was every man for himself.

There was no nest egg set aside for a rainy day. No safety net for women like me. In fact, all I had of value were my two sons and their ability to create wealth for someone else through their hard work.

One night after the boys had gone to bed, as the deadline for the unpaid debt fast approached, I descended into despair. I was looking at a future of complete destitution, of wandering the streets without anyone to care or help. In all likelihood, I would die alone in a gutter, my belly empty and my heart broken for my sons—far from my reach and destroyed by slavery.

That night I was tempted to shake my fist at heaven and say, "My husband and I have served you faithfully, God. Why haven't you come through for us?" In the quiet of my prayers, I sensed I should go to Elisha.

Desperate, and with nowhere else to turn, I sought him out the next day. I told him that a creditor was threatening to remove my sons and claim them as his slaves.

Elisha's first response to my plea wasn't promising. "What shall I do for you?" he asked. It felt like he was throwing up his hands and asking, "What do you expect me to do?"

Then I watched Elisha's countenance change. It was as if God was saying to him, "This woman needs shelter from her creditor. Am I not the God who protects and provides?" Jehovah seemed to plant an idea in Elisha's head, and he quickly asked me, "Tell me—what have you in the house?"

I had already cleaned out every cupboard. The larder was empty. There was nothing left but one small treasure.

I responded, "Your servant has nothing in the house except a jar of oil." But a tiny bit of oil is more than enough in the hands of the God who can multiply our little into his plenty.

Elisha gave me careful instructions: "Go outside, borrow vessels from all your neighbors, empty vessels and not too few. Then go in and shut the door behind yourself and your sons and pour into all these vessels. And when one is full, set it aside."

> **A tiny bit of oil is more than enough in the hands of the God who can multiply our little into his plenty.**

Were Elisha's instructions logical? No. They made little sense. Nonetheless, I didn't wait to obey until I understood.

I didn't brush Elisha off, asking, "Multiplying oil? Really? What's your Plan B?"

Remembering the stories Lemuel told me of God's miraculous power, I did everything Elisha instructed. Amazing, isn't it, how desperate need can make us deeply attentive to God's instructions?

You should have seen my sons' faces when I told them the prophet's plan. But they were good boys and knew to obey.

The three of us went door to door, asking neighbors for any empty vessels they could spare. One by one, jars began to fill our small house, bulging from cabinets, tucked into corners, stacked by descending size on the floor. And then we shut the doors behind us. What God was about to do required privacy, not the prying eyes (and possible mocking) of unbelieving neighbors.

We had but one small jar of precious oil. Rare in a time of famine, it was all the more valuable. I began to pour its contents into the first of the vessels my sons and I had collected. I poured and poured, until the second vessel was nearly full and ready to be set aside.

"Quick, hand me the next!" I instructed. My sons' eyes were alight with wonder.

God was doing something astonishing, and I needed to do my part faithfully. I poured one miraculous jarful of glistening, golden oil after another. My arms ached and my back throbbed as I bent over my labors, but I poured on, and on, and on.

The creditor came knocking on the door—even while I poured. "Only one more day, woman. One more day, and your sons are mine!"

I whispered urgently to my sons in the holy outpouring God was giving us: "Keep handing me the vessels, my sons. Do not delay, for your lives depend on it."

And so they did. From one vessel to the next, my sons handed me every jar we had borrowed. Finally, there were no more to fill. When the flow of oil stopped, my sons and I sat back and whooped with joy. Only Jehovah could have done such a thing!

The next day I returned to Elisha, exclaiming, "It worked! I followed the instructions you gave me, and God supplied abundantly." He rejoiced with me and instructed, "Go, sell the oil and pay your debts, and you and your sons can live on the rest."

God gave my sons and me a powerful provision, a secure refuge for me in widowhood. And in the years that followed, my sons remembered how God worked on their behalf when all other hope was lost.

Miraculous Multiplication

Sister, are you in financial trouble? You may not fear your children being forced into slavery, as the widow of 2 Kings did, but are there other worst-case financial scenarios that swirl through your mind? The loss of a husband incited the widow's problems, but there are so many other catastrophes that can wreak havoc with our finances. Unexpected health-care costs, accidents, job loss, lagging economies— the list could go on. And that's not even touching on the positive blessings that can bring financial strain, such as new children in the family, expenses for educational opportunities, or the cost of beginning a new business or ministry.

Maybe, like the widow in 2 Kings 4, you're staring at an impossible debt that you have no idea how to repay. When financial "famines" hit, they leave us desperately looking for help.

What is the impossible bill that looms before you? Have you come to the end of yourself in trying to fix your financial struggles? But what if the debt you cannot pay is actually a portal into God's sacred refuge? What if that place where you're feeling desperate for provision turns out to be the exact point where God wants to show you his miraculous multiplication?

The widow in 2 Kings had come to the end of her own ideas and solutions. And she didn't understand the logic of Elisha's instructions to gather jars and containers. But rather than hiding from her creditors, she stepped out in faith and followed God's instructions through Elisha. What she found was the refuge of God's provision, beyond what she could have imagined.

Are you ready to step into the sacred refuge God gives you in Jesus?

Sheltered by Jesus, Our Provider

What does the story of the widow, which happened centuries before Christ, say to those of us in dire need of God's protection and provision today? Our cultural backgrounds may be worlds apart, but I believe we have more in common with the widow of 2 Kings 4 than we realize.

She desperately needed the refuge of a perfect Provider and Protector, and she found that in *Jehovah Jireh* (Genesis 22:14). We can take great comfort from her story—seeing an example of God's powerful provision for the practical needs of his people. Her actions remind us to turn to God with our financial concerns—and to trust in his provision. As Paul said in Romans 8:32: "He who did not spare his own Son but gave him up for us all, how will he not also with him graciously give us all things?"

But the widow's acute need points us to a deeper need we share: No matter our financial situation, we all have a debt that undoes us. It is the debt of sin that, if left to our own devices, we could never hope to pay. The same God who faithfully met the widow's need is the One who provided the Lamb of God (see Genesis 22:8; John 1:29; Revelation 5:6). And this Lamb—Jesus Christ our Savior and Lord—paid everything we owe.

The Bill We Cannot Pay

This widow's huge debt stood between her and freedom. It opposed her, stealing her peace. Her debt was mountainous, just like the debt of our sin. Without the help and intervention of God, the woman's unmet obligation would have brought about the dissolution of her family, the end of her security.

Without the intervention of Christ, our unpaid sin debt would have brought not only a lifetime of bondage but also eternal death and separation from God. Referencing the Bible's clear teaching that "the wages of sin is death" (Romans 6:23), Old Testament scholar Ray Dillard says, "The greatest debt we all have is the mortgage on our souls. It is a debt we cannot pay. But God can pay it. He has paid it by giving his own Son as a ransom for our souls."[2]

The widow's crushing debt represents our own sin debt before a holy God. But just as the widow's story wasn't over, ours isn't either.

Knowing his death was imminent, Jesus shared the Passover Feast with his disciples. Holding up the cup of wine, he said, "Drink of it, all of you, for this is my blood of the covenant, which is poured out for many for the forgiveness of sins" (Matthew 26:27–28). John 19:34 tells us that on the cross, not only blood but also water poured out from Jesus's body when he was "pierced for our transgressions" (Isaiah 53:5). Jesus offered up the vessel of his body, and when the Father crushed him in our place, what came forth was blood (to expunge our sins) and water (to wash away our guilt). Jesus allowed his life's essence to be poured and poured and poured, until the sin of God's people was paid for. The debt now completely covered, the flow stopped. And it will never be needed again.

TRANSFORMING TRUTH

Fear keeps us up at night with, "You got yourself into this mess; it's up to you to get out of it." But God's generous mercy speaks a better word: "Bring your debts to me, and ask me to do what you cannot do for yourself. Beloved, I am with you in this."

In 1876 Robert Lowry penned the famous hymn "Nothing But the Blood," its words a beautiful picture of our debt forever washed away:

> What can wash away my sin?
> Nothing but the blood of Jesus;
> What can make me whole again?
> Nothing but the blood of Jesus.
> Oh! Precious is the flow
> That makes me white as snow;
> No other fount I know,
> Nothing but the blood of Jesus.[3]

Everything We Need

I'll be honest. I sometimes miss the distinction between what I need and what I want. I blur the line. And let's just say my list of wants can be long.

Can you relate? Sometimes, when we have confused needs with wants, what we are really afraid of isn't whether God will provide what we need, but that we won't get what we want. We can trust that even if God doesn't give us what we want, it's for a reason, and he will *always* provide what we need for each moment. Above all, he promises—and delivers—the provision of his forgiving love and presence.

If we have bought into the world's assertion that our value comes from what we own, we often hide our weaknesses and insecurities by finding identity in money or the things it can buy. Or perhaps we expend a lot of effort hiding our needs from others, feeling ashamed. No matter where we fall on the financial spectrum, money can become a way we hide from God's work in our lives. Are you ready to jump off the hamster wheel—that hopeless cycle of trying to get and be "enough"?

Thankfully, God's promise to provide goes deeper than our bank accounts! He's paid the price for our sin struggles with the life of his only Son—which means we can always renew our commitment to trust in him. And surely if he would pay our sin debts with his very life, we can trust him to help with our financial debts as well.

Sister, you can come out of hiding, from rooting your identity in money and acquiring "stuff." Right now you can step into the refuge of being God's beloved daughter for whom he promises to provide.

Enter the Sacred Refuge of Jesus, Our Provider

Jesus may be saying something like this to you:

> I saw you there, beloved. In over your head and drowning in a debt that threatened to undo you. Alone, exposed, afraid— you were about to lose it all. There was nothing, short of your very life, you could offer to pay what you owed.
>
> I did it for you.
>
> When you had no idea where to turn, at just the right time the Father made full provision for your debt through me. When you had nothing in your hands to give, no ability to pay, I provided the cleansing flow of my blood. The death warranted by your unmet debt became my death. And as my blood flowed, covering your sin, I also gave you my full righteousness. Beloved, you went from being a wretched pauper living under a death sentence to a blood-bought child of our Father, delightful in his eyes.
>
> My sacrifice accomplished once and for all what the sacrifice of bulls and goats could not. It washed away the law's ability to condemn you to death. My blood—poured out lavishly for you—*bought* you back to life. And the power of my blood provides not just any life; it restores to you a life of abundance, for you and your household.
>
> Beloved, let me ask you this: how many jars have you collected? That is, how much do you trust me to provide for your needs fully and even lavishly? Elisha, directed by my Spirit, instructed the widow to gather "not a few" jars in which to

receive the abundant flow of oil. She sold it all, paid her debts, and lived on the rest.

Is it possible you understand that I have paid your sin debt, but do not fully grasp—or trust—that you no longer need to live like you are still "in debt"? Once having been freed, have you become enslaved again to fear, distraction, idols, insecurities, or disbelief?

Beloved, how much do you trust me to provide for your needs fully and even lavishly?

Put this mindset and practice behind you, dear one, for it is the Father's will not only that you trust the flow of my blood to cancel your sin debt but also that you live on the riches I have given you. Having paid the debt you could not pay, I have also given you "every spiritual blessing in the heavenly places." Your days of living in oppression, fear, or anxiety—even when you don't know what the outcome of a situation will be—are over.

Are you tired and overwhelmed by heavy financial responsibilities? I invite you to take shelter in me, for I never grow weary, and I have promised "[renewed] strength" to the exhausted. Have you become entangled in the sin of distraction so that you no longer have time for God's Word? As your Provider, I call you to shelter in my full forgiveness and in the richness of his Word that will fill up your life (your empty jars) with life-giving, soul-nourishing sweetness. And once you have tasted the real thing, you will not settle for less.

This is an important time to take stock of your life. Ask for more of my Spirit and the ability to see yourself as you really are. Perhaps there is a part of you that thinks, *Actually, I'm doing okay. I am rich, I have prospered, and I need nothing.* But you may not realize that you are "wretched, pitiable, poor, blind, and naked." If you are depending on your own meager resources, beloved, then "I counsel you to buy from me gold refined by fire, so that you may be rich, and white garments so that you may clothe yourself and the shame of your nakedness may not be seen, and salve to anoint your eyes, so that you may see." Dear one, I only reprove those I love.

Come to me, and enter the flow of my love, my cleansing blood, and the oil of my Spirit to heal you. The provision is perfect. The protection is complete. The shelter of my blood will hold.[4]

REST Under His Wings
Spend time quieting yourself in God's presence.

Release control.
1. What is happening in your life right now financially? Are you in any financial trouble?
2. Have you fallen for the bigger, better, newer trap so prevalent in our culture? Where has it led you?
3. In what ways have you tried to fix your own debts or financial struggles? Do you feel ready to release control of the situation into God's hands? Why or why not?

Father, I now release control of my finances into your hands. I ask you to guide me out of debt and into financial freedom.

Exchange your *unpayable debt* for the shelter of Christ's *provision.*
4. How do you view your spiritual debt before God? How would you describe the status of that bill? Outstanding? Overdue? Paid in full?

5. In what ways have you tried to hide your sin debt from God or deal with it on your own? What would it look like for you to exchange that debt for the shelter of Jesus's provision?

Father, I have hidden from you, aware that I cannot be "good enough" on my own. I now come out of hiding and ask you to make a path for me back into your presence.

See yourself in union with Christ.

6. What practical step could you take to seek God's presence when you feel overwhelmed by debt—whether it be the weight of finances or the weight of sin?

Father, I am so grateful that Jesus paid my debt for sin and gave me freedom before you. Having been set free, please help me to live free.

Trust Christ as the one who shelters you in his provision.

7. Create a breath prayer (for example: "Father . . . I depend on you." Or "Jesus . . . you are enough." Or "Jehovah Jireh . . . my Provider"). You can pray this moment by moment as you continue to walk out of hiding and into the sheltering presence of God, your Provider.

CHAPTER 6

Rescued

Finding Shelter in Christ's Mercy

Be merciful to me, O God, be merciful to me,
for in you my soul takes refuge;
in the shadow of your wings I will take refuge,
till the storms of destruction pass by.
—PSALM 57:1

Can God give someone with my past a new beginning?

SEVERAL YEARS AGO, I taught a women's retreat for a church in the South. During that retreat, I sent the women out to spend time with God in prayer. One woman I'll call Catherine approached me and asked if we could talk. I sensed urgency in her voice.

As we walked along the edge of a quiet lake, her story tumbled out. With tears welling in her eyes, Catherine told me about what happened to her during college. She was an orphan and not a believer at the time. She had earned some scholarships and had worked hard to put herself through college. But the summer before her senior year tuition was due, funding was cut and she lost her scholarship. A friend of Catherine's told her about a quick way to raise funds: sleep with guys willing to pay for her time. At first, Catherine was repulsed by the idea. However, with a tuition bill looming before her, she eventually decided to give it a try.

That summer she lived a double life and raised enough money to start her final year of college. She finished school, married (a man who knew nothing about her past), and started a family. But years later, still feeling dirty and overwhelmed by what she had done, she attempted to make up for her past.

Crushed by guilt she couldn't shake, Catherine sought shelter in perfectionism and self-effort. Her home had to be immaculate. She had to be the best mom on the planet. She had to run every children's program at her local church. When I met Catherine, she was completely exhausted and knew her life wasn't working.

Further, the enemy had used this secret sin to tell Catherine, "God is still angry with you and will judge you for what you did. The fact that you sold your body to the highest bidder makes you a second-class citizen in his household. And you might as well forget your dreams of serving the Lord. Your broken past disqualifies you from ever being used by him in ministry."

But the Lord was wooing Catherine during the women's retreat. He had come to rescue her, offering her the radical freedom of the gospel. And as we sat and talked, the Holy Spirit drew us into prayer. I watched as Catherine finally relinquished the shame of prostitution *and* her pathological perfectionism. She received full forgiveness, knowing she was completely restored to the Father who loved her.

Then the Holy Spirit did something more for her. I will never forget his mercy.

As Catherine confessed that she hadn't believed God could truly forgive her, an unholy afterbirth of old, fetid lies (based on condemnation, self-hatred, and shame) came forth from her spirit. But God did not leave her empty. I watched as he planted something new and powerful in the womb of her spirit. It was a glorious exchange and a fresh birth of something completely new in Catherine's life!

One year later, as we gathered for a third annual retreat, Catherine came bounding up to me, her face shining.

"What a year it's been," she exclaimed. "You won't believe what God's been doing!"

Over lunch her story emerged. She had been able to bring her past to her husband and ask for his forgiveness. Because of their shared relationship with Christ, he was able to forgive her and treat her as clean and shameless. Now freed from the lie that God was still angry with her and that her old sin disqualified her from ministry, Catherine had followed God's call to start sharing her past with others, especially young women with sexually broken stories.

As she did so, God brought women to her who were still struggling

with their pasts. Catherine launched a ministry of healing and restoration for women like herself—who had not been able to trust God's
forgiveness or forgive themselves. I have rarely seen someone so full
of joy and purpose as Catherine. The "scene of the crime," the very
place the enemy said sidelined Catherine from ministry, had become
the source of God's calling in her life.

Disqualified by Our Past?

Catherine's story causes me to ask: "What if Satan is dead wrong?
What if you don't have to try harder to win God's approval? What if
past sin, forgiven by God, doesn't disqualify you from ministry but can
actually become the source of your life's true purpose?"

I wonder if those are questions your heart is asking as well?

Here's the hope-filled answer God provides: because of Jesus's work
on the cross, your past doesn't have to be a stain on the present. In fact,
God can birth something new and beautiful from that past pain. The
apostle Paul (once Saul), who had once persecuted and killed followers of Jesus Christ before his own conversion, put it this way: "But one
thing I do: forgetting what lies behind and straining forward to what
lies ahead, I press on toward the goal for the prize of the upward call of
God in Christ Jesus" (Philippians 3:13–14).

Sister, what is the past sin you can't quite believe God has forgiven?
How have you dealt with it? By overcompensating? Hiding in self-
effort? Maybe, like Catherine, you've been trying so hard to build a
perfect, unblemished life, all the while doubting that God has really
removed the stain of sin from your past.

How is that going for you? Are you weary from the constant juggling of activities, from the niggling doubts that never quite leave your
heart at peace? Living with the weight of your past grows exhausting,
doesn't it? Are you ready to relinquish the lie "I can rescue myself"?

What if your past, redeemed by God, turned out to be an unexpected
path forward into a life you have never imagined possible? That's exactly what our ancient sister Rahab, whose story unfolds in the book

of Joshua, discovered to be true. Her life answers the question so many of us continue to struggle with: "Can God give someone with my past a new beginning?"

Rahab's Story

Canaan, the land where Rahab lived, was inhabited by a group of pagan tribes. We know them as the "ites"—the Canaanites, Jebusites, Girgashites, Hittites, Hivites, Perizzites, and Amorites. This last people group inhabited the region west of the Jordan River and settled in or near the fortified city of Jericho, a city of about three thousand at the time of Joshua.

Amorite culture was obsessed with power, wealth, and prosperity. The inhabitants of Jericho worshiped a pantheon—a group of gods— often through ritual sex and child sacrifice. Ray Vander Laan explains, "Their worshipers engaged in immoral sex to cause the gods to join together, ensuring good harvests. This practice became the basis for religious prostitution (1 Kings 14:23–24). The priest or a male member of the community represented Baal. The priestess or a female member of the community represented Asherah. In this way, God's incredible gift of sexuality was perverted to the most obscene public prostitution."[1]

By the time of Joshua, when the Amorites' wickedness had reached its fullness, God was ready to judge them, to eradicate the debauchery of these pagan people and fulfill his promise to establish his people in the land of Canaan.

With our modern sensibility, we may struggle to understand why God wiped out a whole city (the first of many). Isn't he a God of love? He is, but he is also a God of holiness and justice: he has "mercy on whomever he wills, and he hardens whomever he wills" (Romans 9:18).

In the story of one extraordinary Amorite woman named Rahab, we encounter a God through whom mercy triumphs over judgment. Her story echoes in our own question: *Can God give someone with my past a new beginning?*

Rahab lived in the oldest city in the world, practicing what some have called the oldest profession. Her story, which occurred around 1450 BC, unfolds in Joshua 2 and Joshua 6:15–25. I encourage you to take time to read these passages.

This remarkable woman, who began her life as a pagan prostitute, is also mentioned in three New Testament passages. How could her influence reach so far? Because by faith in Jehovah's power to save her, she received Christ's sacred refuge. God sheltered a heathen harlot in mercy—and raised her up as a mighty mother of faith among his people.

If Rahab were to tell us her story of sacred refuge, it might sound something like this:

I hadn't planned on selling my body for money. But when my mother and father fell on hard times and the little ones cried because their bellies were empty, I saw no other way. For me it was simple: either serve as a prostitute in the temple of Baal-Hadad, go into business for myself, or marry. With no suitor on the horizon and time running out, I did what I had to do.

Trick by trick, brick by brick, I built a shelter for us, protecting us from hunger and want. Jericho was a military outpost, so I had no lack of customers. In the mornings I used to sit at my window embedded in the city wall, enjoying the view of the low-slung mountains to the east. I would call out to passersby, drumming up business. I won't lie: I did well for myself. Men knew the way to "Rahab's house."

Women, of course, shunned me. From the moment I hung up my shingle, I became invisible to them, a stranger to those who used to be friends. To them, I was a bottom-feeder, an outsider to polite society. Over time, I came to hate my life, and even myself. I was used, and a user. I felt my life slipping away, like there was less and less of me each day. And so to protect myself, I put up walls—as thick as the walls of Jericho—around my heart. I hid there until the day I overheard several customers talking. One of them ended the discussion with this:

"I know Jericho's walls are thicker than anyone else's, but I think we're in serious trouble here. Now that their army has crossed the river, where will that leave us? Their god Jehovah goes into battle with them. How do you beat an army whose god fights for them? I mean, how do you survive that?"

For years I had heard the stories about this god Jehovah and the people whom he loved and protected. Now the whole city was melting with fear because the Israelites had crossed the river and entered the region. As I listened to this conversation, something new began to form in me. Was it fear? Yes, I was afraid of a god powerful enough to do all this for those who worshiped him. The fact that he was the god of a nation other than mine . . . well, that filled me with dread for my city and my family. But it was more than that.

When everyone else in Jericho lost heart and the will to fight, a sure knowledge began to grow in me that not only was Jehovah the true God, but he might become *my* God.

You can't do the work I did without building walls around your heart. They were formed from my own self-effort and determination: "I can rescue myself. If I work hard enough, I can save myself and my family." Now something, or someone, was beginning to shake those walls.

Not long afterward, two outsiders ambled into my establishment, trying to look like they belonged there. My inner radar hit high alert. Something was different about these men. They were shabby compared to many of my other customers. Could they pay?

It turned out they weren't interested in my services, just in a place to stay. That was a new one!

The more I observed them, the more I began to suspect

these men weren't who they said they were—farmers who had come to Jericho to sell their surplus produce at the city's market. Perhaps they were Israelites sent to spy out the city. A plan began to form in my mind. This was the chance I had longed for: to escape the judgment I knew was coming to Jericho.

When everyone else in Jericho lost the will to fight, a sure knowledge began to grow in me that not only was Jehovah the true God, but he might become *my* God.

Sensing their need for secrecy, I offered them sleeping quarters on the roof for the night, and even concealed them under flax. Later that night, when the king's men, alerted by a tip, came banging on my door for the two men, I surprised even myself. I lied for them and even misdirected the king's men. Sure, it was a big risk, but something told me this was the way to go.

Later when I went up to the roof to check on them, the men were relieved but perplexed. It was time to make a stand. I told them what I'd come to believe: "I know the Lord has given you the land. Our hearts are melting in fear before you and your God. We've heard how the Lord dried up the water of the Red Sea when you came out of Egypt. We know what you did to the two kings of the Amorites who were beyond the Jordan, to Sihon and Og. You destroyed them, and not a child nor a baby lamb was spared. I tell you this: these stories have caused our hearts to melt like wax. There is no spirit left in any man because of you, for the Lord your God, he is God in the heavens above and on the earth beneath."

How had I come to know this? Who can say? All I know is that I was beginning to see things through a different lens. I wasn't in control of my life anymore. I was a small part of what their God was doing.

The men looked at each other like deer caught within range of the archer. Had I figured out who they were? Should they pretend not to understand, or might this be God at work on their behalf? Just trying to disappear, these Israelite spies had ducked down a dark alley and found their way to my house.

There was nothing for them to do but trust me. They knew I held their lives in my hands. But my life—and that of my family—was also on the line. I was a business woman. So I proposed an arrangement that would benefit us all.

"Let's make a deal. Swear to me by the Lord that, just as I have saved your hides from the king's men, you also will deal kindly with my family. I need you to give me a sure sign that you will save my father and mother, my brothers and sisters, and our whole household, from death."

I had provided shelter for them; now I asked for shelter in return.

I admit I was surprised when the men said to me, "We're in. We pledge our lives for yours! If you don't tell the king about this business of ours, then when the Lord gives us the land, we will be sure to spare you and your family."

It was done. I came to realize later that the agreement I made that day with the spies was actually an agreement with their God. It guaranteed a refuge for my family and me from that day on.

I told the men to hide in the hills, where the pursuers wouldn't find them. Because my house was built into the city wall, I let them down by a rope through a window. And then the men gave me the most extraordinary instructions. True to their word, they gave me the sign I asked for:

"Rahab, if you want us to be faithful to our end of the bargain, tie this scarlet cord in the window through which you let us down. Then gather your whole household together and do not leave your home. If anyone goes out of the doors of your house into the street, his blood will be on his own head. Don't hold us responsible for what happens to him. If a hand is laid on anyone who is with you in the house, the fault will be ours. But this agreement only holds if you keep the secret about us."

I said, "So be it."

Immediately after the spies left, I tied the scarlet cord in the window. I was taking no chances. If the cord could carry the men away to safety, it would work for my family and me on the day of invasion.

Our city was large—with about three thousand citizens when the Israelites came to conquer the land. We had spent considerable effort and expense building city walls that exceeded any others in height and thickness. No army had been able to breach or scale them, but I had ceased to trust in our city's walls to save us from the Israelites' attack.

A few days later, we woke to the sound of horns blaring and the steady beat of thousands of men marching toward Jericho. Every citizen of the city huddled behind our massive walls as approximately six hundred thousand fighting men marched around our city.

Once, twice, three times . . . Israel marched along the city's perimeter until the soldiers had completed seven circuits around Jericho's walls. Each circuit wound our stomachs into a tighter knot of terror. I eyed the scarlet cord, tied securely at the window. Would it protect us from destruction?

The blast of rams' horns cut the eerie silence inside Jericho. And then we heard a new noise—the paean of thousands of voices crying out to Jehovah for victory.

A great *crack* broke forth as the city's walls began to shatter.

One fissure formed just beyond where my house was built inside the wall.

> ## I eyed the scarlet cord, tied securely at the window. Would it protect us from destruction?

Strangely, the walls of Jericho didn't crumble into a heap. Instead, we watched in horror as they toppled down flat, creating an access ramp for each man in the Israelite army to march right into the city laid open before him. It was a day of dread and destruction. Crouched down safely in our house, my family and I heard the agonizing cries of our neighbors as they were crushed by the falling wall.

But it was also a day of rescue and relief. My house, marvelously, remained untouched. The hand of the Israelites' God must have hovered above it, sheltering us. Just as the spies had promised, the scarlet cord placed as a sign at our window protected us while the rest of my city was totally demolished.

Chaos and mayhem surrounded us. We heard cries of alarm and violence above and below. Thick dust swirled everywhere, making it hard to see just a few feet ahead of us.

Heading to the exterior wall, which was still miraculously intact, I could just make out our scarlet cord tied to the window. A beacon of hope, it directed the spies to our house. I gathered my family, and we followed closely after the Israelite spies as they brought us safely out of the city.

As we escaped the city's destruction and could breathe again, I uttered this prayer, "God of the Israelites, great and mighty one, I thank you for rescuing me and those I care for.

Guide our steps forward. Protect and provide for us, even as you have this day."

He did. All I had asked of the spies was a safe exit from Jericho for myself and my family. But Jehovah and his people did immeasurably more for us. At first, my family and I lived outside the camp. In time, the people came to accept us. They knew we had rejected our Amorite roots and thrown our lot in with them.

Later, God blessed me with more beautiful beginnings. I married a high-ranking Jewish man, which no one (including me) dreamed could be possible. And God allowed me to birth our precious son Boaz, who grew into a fine man of noble character.

All because I trusted in that scarlet cord and left my crumbling walls behind.

Trusting the Scarlet Cord

It cost Rahab everything to trust in the spies' scarlet cord. Her faith in Jehovah's provision of the cord reminds me of my own "Come to Jesus" moment.

During my twenties, I served as a volunteer leader with Young Life. One summer we brought a group of high school students from New Jersey to Frontier Ranch in Colorado. One of our challenges was to experience rappelling as a faith-building exercise.

It turned out God wanted to grow *my* faith. I still remember the fear that held me hostage as I led the girls in my cabin up the side of a high hill with a sheer cliff face. This was where we would descend from! My job was to show the girls rappelling was safe, so I went first, strapping into the harness, connecting myself to the red belaying rope, and stepping off the cliff face—backward.

They say, "Don't look down." They're right. The moment I looked behind me down the face of that two-hundred-foot cliff, fear paralyzed me. Trying to navigate backward down that wall of stone while staying upright nearly cost me my life (or at least my knees)!

There came a point when I had to put my full trust in the thick cord that held my weight. I had to remember that it was anchored securely to the tree at the top of the cliff. As I did so, my whole orientation began to change. By shifting my full weight backward and trusting the rope to hold me, I began to experience an exhilarating freedom as I traversed the cliff all the way to the ground.

Later that day as I was processing this experience with the Lord, I realized I had spent years pretending to trust Jesus's payment for my past, when in reality I had been playing "Let's Make a Deal" with God. It went something like this: "If I become the perfect wife/mom/daughter/pastor's wife/neighbor/employee, you'll have to come through for me, God, and excuse my past indiscretions." It's a deal God never would or could agree to. Why? Because, according to the gospel, he has done for us what we could never do for ourselves: he has exchanged our sinfulness for Christ's righteousness.

TRANSFORMING TRUTH

Self-effort drives you forward with, "It's all up to you. You are on your own. There are no free rides, so get at it!" God's grace gentles you with, "Beloved, on your own, you will never be able to make up for your past mistakes. But I am with you, and I have spilled my own blood to rescue you from destruction."

Let me ask, sister, what sin in your past story still has the power to make you feel ashamed? Are you still trying to manage your own sin? Have you been hiding behind walls of self-reliance, trying to protect yourself from God's wrath? Or have you been on a long campaign of earning God's good opinion by trying to be a perfect wife or parent or employee or caregiver?

Have you tried to become your own savior, cultivating a perfect appearance through constant diets and overexercise, or through over-working that leads to achievement and admiration?

What would it look like for you to let those walls of self-reliance come crashing down—to trust God's love to hold you, even as your messy, imperfect self? What if you could trust, once and for all, that God doesn't expect you to save yourself? What if the same scarlet cord that carried Rahab to safety can carry you all the way into the safe refuge of God's waiting arms?

Sheltered by Jesus, Our Propitiation

Rahab asked the spies for a "sure sign" that they would be faithful to save her and her family when the invasion began. The Hebrew word for "sign" can also be translated as "pledge" or "token." She was asking for a sign of good faith in the bargain they had struck—on which all their lives depended.

We have seen a symbol like this before. In Exodus 12:13, God gave his people a "sure sign," also red in color, that they would be protected from death. On the last night Israel spent in Egypt, God's people placed the blood of lambs on the lintels of their houses, trusting it would spare them from the angel of death. The sign the spies gave Rahab, the scarlet cord, pointed unmistakably to the blood of Jesus Christ, shed for her sin, and ours.

In trusting this sign, Rahab stepped out of her past as an unworthy outsider into a shimmering new destiny as one made worthy by faith in Jehovah, who would make propitiation for her sins by the blood of his Son.

But what exactly is *propitiation*? It may sound like an intimidating or old-time word, but it's such an important idea to understand, so let's look at what it means. *Propitiation* is the action taken that causes someone or something "to become favorably inclined; [to] win or regain the goodwill of; [to] appease," such as an atoning sacrifice.[2]

This concept is at the heart of Christ's work for us! He appeased *all* the wrath of God aimed at our sin. Jesus *became* our sin, turning

God's anger and condemnation away from us forever. In the garden of Gethsemane, Jesus asked that he not have to drink from the cup of the Father's wrath. But on the cross, Jesus didn't just sip from the cup of the Father's anger against our sin; he drank it to the lees. There is no more wrath left for us!

This same Jesus "was crushed for our iniquities; upon him was the chastisement that brought us peace" (Isaiah 53:5). Jesus was crushed for Rahab—and all who put their faith in his blood—so that she could receive God's mercy.

Rahab's faith points to a future Savior who would be crushed for her transgressions so that she could be spared the same death as her neighbors in Jericho. By asking for—and trusting in—this sign, Rahab shifted her allegiance from the worship of pagan deities to the worship of Jehovah, whom she acknowledged fully in Joshua 2:11: "The LORD your God, he is God in the heavens above and on the earth beneath."

> ### Jesus didn't just sip from the cup of the Father's anger against our sin; he drank it to the lees. There is no more wrath left for us!

The testimony of Scripture is that Jesus became our sin, leaving us with *no sin*, to stand before God as our true selves, the people he originally created us to be. Because of Rahab's faith, God did this for her as well. Her final identity in Scripture isn't as a prostitute, but as a grandmother in the lineage of Jesus—the true woman God created her to be. Just as God rewrote Rahab's story, he stands ready to rewrite yours. Your sin-scarred past, sister, does not have to be your shameful secret anymore. It can be a portal through which God invites you to follow him into a glorious new life where you are free to serve him and others.

What Are You Trusting to Shelter You?

Everyone in Jericho that day hoped that their mighty walls would keep Israel out. What about you? Do you sometimes trust in walls to protect and preserve your own life?

What have you put your confidence in apart from Christ? What have you thought would protect, uphold, and define you other than God? Although these false shelters look strong and trustworthy, in reality they are strongholds. In 2 Corinthians 10:4–5 Paul talks about destroying spiritual strongholds, houses of thought erected brick by brick as we believe lies "raised against the knowledge of God." But these strongholds are also demolished as we "take every thought captive to obey Christ." As he did for Rahab, God offers to rescue you from the futility of trusting in walls destined to fall.

Jehovah sent his people to invade Jericho in judgment for the city's sin and in fulfillment of his promise to give the land to Israel. But he also sent them there to rescue one woman and her family. He knocked down the walls of an entire city to bring her into his true shelter.

Even now he has also come to rescue you, sister. In fact, God may be using a crisis that is dredging up your past to help you experience your greatest longings fulfilled: to be fully known, fully seen, and *still* fully loved. God may be allowing your walls to crumble as the means of experiencing his rescue and refuge.

As you trust him, it will be the beginning of a whole new identity and life for you.

Broken Beginnings Become Beautiful Endings

Rahab's story teaches us that God is powerful enough to redeem any of our stories, and he is good enough to use us as his life-givers for others. What about you? What has the enemy told you disqualifies you from being used by God? Don't believe it, sister! Just as it was for our sacred sister Catherine, the very brokenness of your past—redeemed by Jesus Christ and put at his disposal—can become the compass to your future ministry to others! As it was for Catherine and Rahab, your past mistakes, forgiven and redeemed by God, can become the fuel that propels you into a whole new chapter of your life.

Perhaps you can relate to Rahab, broken by sexual sin and an outcast from polite society or "nice" church people. Perhaps you are hiding behind walls of your own making, false shelters that are starting to crumble.

I connect with Rahab as someone who has also hidden behind walls of shame. Several years ago during a time of prayer, I realized that I avoided talking to God unless I could come to him feeling good about myself and all my accomplishments for him. If I wasn't feeling good about my recent performance, then my posture before the Lord was one of holding my hands in front of my face as I spoke with him.

For years, I held God at arm's length, hiding my true face, my real self, before him, still waiting for the other shoe to drop for sins in my college years. By not completely trusting in his forgiveness (and in not forgiving myself), I had missed out on the full pardon he gives us in Christ: being fully seen and still fully loved.

That day God rescued me from trying to be my own savior and protector. My hands fell away from my face, and it was a turning point in our relationship. I began to experience sacred refuge with him: deeper trust and intimacy.

Sister, are you ready for your own turning point with God? Are you exhausted from carrying the burdens of your past? Even now, God is inviting you to throw all that weight onto the scarlet rope of Jesus's mercy.

It's a rope that will always hold.

Enter the Sacred Refuge of Christ's Mercy

Through his Spirit Jesus may be encouraging you right now with words like these:

> I see you there, beloved, standing at the window of your prison
> cell, looking out. Your past is pockmarked with the devastation

caused by sin—yours and others against you. How you long to be rescued, to be invited to the table of deep fellowship with me and others in my household. But your past keeps holding you back.

You know that justice must be served. Payment must be made. Wrath must be appeased.

Beloved, here is good news for you: It has been. The just payment for your sin has been made. As your Savior, I completely removed the Father's anger at your sin. As you come to trust this, you will also begin to believe that we are not chronically disappointed in you.

I did not go to the cross and suffer my Father's rejection so you would live in bondage to your past, your failures, or your attempts to atone for them yourself. I laid down my life so you could take up yours!

But you have spent so many years rehearsing your failures and trying to make up for them. With your eyes on your past instead of fixed on me, you have believed the lie that I could never use someone as broken as you.

Will you, once and for all, relinquish what is over and done with? It is not your true identity. Will you give me all the broken pieces of your past and watch me create something useful and life-giving out of it all? In my kingdom, broken beginnings become beautiful endings. Even now, I am rewriting your story.

But we will only get there together as you fully release the past and press on toward the future I have planned. Beloved, are you ready to stop hiding behind walls of self-effort and performance? It's time to leave the prison of your own making and enter my shelter.

Do you not know that you are lovely and flawless in my sight? Beloved, do you see the strong refuge I have given you?

It is established on the unshakable foundation of my righteousness received by faith.

Look up and you will see that a strong roof, constructed of my mercy, covers you. Look closely and you will see my blood posted on the lintels of the doorway. Dear one, the sacred refuge of my mercy and grace is built for you. It is time to come in.[3]

REST Under His Wings

Spend time quieting yourself in God's presence.

Release control.
1. Are there past struggles or mistakes that you still think about a lot?
2. In what ways have you been hiding from God through self-effort? What form has that taken?
3. How have these attempts to be your own savior added to the weight you carry?

Father, I come to you now covered in Jesus's righteousness, and confess that I am not my own savior. You are. I now release my need to appease your wrath through performance.

Exchange your *self-effort* for the shelter of Christ's *propitiation*.
4. Do you struggle to believe in propitiation—that Jesus took all your sin on himself so that God now sees your righteousness in Christ, not your past sin? If so, how does this affect the way you think about your past—and your future?
5. In what ways do your self-efforts reveal a lack of trust in God?

Father, please forgive me for trying to manage my sin through hiding from it in self-effort. Right now I ask you to help me come fully out of hiding and to enter freely into your presence and shelter. I trust that you have dealt decisively with my sinful past, turning away your former wrath against me.

See yourself in union with Christ.

6. What part of your past have you felt disqualifies you from God's ability to use you? As he did for Catherine, how might God use someone with your past to reach others with a similar story? Ask God to help you live in light of your union with Christ—so that others can see him through you.

Father, I trust that you have a hope and a future for me. Would you—once and for all—carry me out of a past marked by spiritual death and into your redeemed purposes for me as a life-giver? Help me see myself as you see me: your beloved, blood-bought child. I believe that you can use anyone to accomplish your purposes—even me. Please show me in the days ahead what that might look like.

Trust Christ as your propitiation.

7. Create a breath prayer response to the Lord (for example: "Father . . . I have your favor. Jesus . . . you are enough." Or "Jesus, I release my past . . . so I can receive the future you have for me"). You can pray this breath prayer moment by moment as you continue to walk out of hiding and into God's sheltering presence.

CHAPTER 7

Redeemed

Finding Shelter in Your Kinsman-Redeemer

I cry to you, O Lord;
I say, "You are my refuge,
my portion in the land of the living."
—Psalm 142:5

Can I still come home, even when I've wandered from God?

On a cold December night many years ago, our family experienced a life-changing incident. I was fourteen at the time. We had already lost two fathers to divorce and were barely surviving financially. Our crisis hit, from an earthly perspective, at the worst possible moment.

My mother was driving my younger brother, sister, and me home from Christmas shopping one dark New England night. Our car hit a huge sheet of black ice, spinning us out of control. My mother was severely injured.

While the paramedics were loading her into the ambulance, she got word to me to "call the Baileys," a newly retired couple in our church. They had taken our broken family under their wing and loved us well.

The flashing lights vanished, and the siren drifted into silence as my mother was rushed to the ER on that frozen night. The police placed my brother, my sister, and me in the back of a cruiser and drove us to the local police station. From there, I called the Baileys as my mother had instructed, choking out the news: "An accident . . . mom hurt badly . . . not sure where they've taken her . . . no place to go."

A strained but comforting voice on the other side of the line said simply, "We'll be right there."

My twelve-year-old brother, four-year-old sister, and I were still in shock and not processing well. But I remember a moment of relief from sickening panic when we arrived at the Baileys' home. Those dear people had turned on every light in the place. Each window shone out as beacons of hope and warmth into the inky night with this simple message: "You are safe. You will be sheltered here."

And we were. As we crossed the threshold out of what felt like an alternate reality into their home, we were met by a crackling fire in the colonial hearth.

After we shared our story, the Baileys ministered to us in the most extraordinary way. With Evan on one side and Mary on the other, they surrounded the three of us with their arms and began to pray. I do not remember their words, but I do remember this: I knew I was safe. I felt sheltered. And I knew everything was going to be okay, because the Lord had not abandoned us. He was with us. He had placed us in the middle of his people.

My siblings and I were welcomed that night—and for the next six months—into the heart of the Bailey family. We had already lost two fathers. Five days later, my mother lost her left leg and, with it, her sense of self. But at the most vulnerable moment in our young lives, the Baileys' home became a sacred refuge for us, a true shelter from the storm that threatened to capsize our family.

Far from Home

Any crisis can be terrifying, but that childhood car accident felt especially jarring because we were away from the safety of our home. It's a feeling I would experience again later during my college years, only this time I'd distanced myself from my spiritual home. I eventually found myself feeling scared and disoriented, just like my fourteen-year-old self. And just as he did after the accident through the Baileys, God invited me to come back to my true home in him.

What about you, sister? Has your life ever been upended by loss? Have you ever felt like you've lost your way—wandering from your relationship with God? Maybe you're in that place right now. Perhaps an overwhelming crisis, or just the ongoing battle of everyday struggles, has caused bitterness and frustration to seep into your heart. It feels like nothing will ever change and God's forgotten about you.

Maybe you're wondering, *Can there really be a happy ending to this story?*

During the night of my family's accident, as my siblings and I piled into that police cruiser for the ride to the station, we had no clue how our story was going to turn out. Our dads were gone. Extended family lived a thousand miles away. All we had was our local church, including the Baileys. But our local church was enough because they surrounded and supported us with the faithful love of God. To this day, I feel the effects of their stabilizing love and faithful protection.

Sometimes crisis happens even when we are closest to God. We can't discern any area of life where we are disobeying him or need loving correction. Other times, though, we may face crises because of our wandering hearts. When life brings about confusion and loss, it's tempting to doubt God's goodness and instead settle into cynicism. It's easy to listen to the voice telling us to just live for ourselves, because surely God has forgotten about us.

But God never forgets his beloved ones. And sometimes crisis brings with it an extraordinary invitation from God to draw closer or return to him.

I wonder, sister, what losses *you* have experienced. What's happened to make you feel far from God? Is it possible that embedded in these struggles is an invitation to return to wholehearted dependence on God and his way? Let's meet a sacred sister whose story answers the question we all ask at one time or another: "Can I still come home, even when I've wandered from God?"

Naomi's Story

I spent two summers in Kenya during my college years, which coincided with a devastating famine across the Horn of Africa that caused thousands of people to migrate. Across the planet today, the same story unfolds. I have seen refugees in Uganda struggling to survive far from their home. Whether because of war, persecution, or famine, families leave their homes in search of food, security, and a better life.

The Scriptures are full of stories of such people on the move. One of the best-known narratives concerns the lives of two refugee women, Ruth and her mother-in-law Naomi. They remind us that in a fallen world, we are all refugees, exiled from our true home and hungry for a place to belong.

Ruth and Naomi were two women who sheltered one another in a sacred sisterhood. Together they experienced the powerful refuge God gives us in his people (including a kinsman-redeemer, a concept we'll explore more deeply in these pages).

In a fallen world, we are all refugees, exiled from our true home and hungry for a place to belong.

Read the book of Ruth in just one sitting if you can—it's just four chapters—to grasp the movement of the story. It is extraordinary for several reasons. First, it is one of only two books in the Bible named after a woman. Second, that woman is not an Israelite, but a pagan. As such, the book of Ruth reveals that God delights to bring the least likely among us into his great story of redemption. That includes you, sister, and me.

Ruth stands as another striking picture of God's work in someone who is an outsider to Israel. Her story was probably written as a corrective to Israel, who was walking away from God at the time. Ruth shows us extraordinary courage, faithfulness, and trust in God.

But for now, I want to focus on Naomi's story. Because Naomi reminds me of the person I am all too often: unfaithful, running from discipline, and pretty sure I can run my life better than God can.

Naomi's story unfolds in the time of the Judges, when "everyone

did what was right in his own eyes" (Judges 21:25). Like the ancient
Hebrew readers, who would remember the biblical backdrop of blessings and curses in Deuteronomy 28–30, we should recognize that Israel was experiencing famine because the people were living as they
saw fit, apart from God. The family of Elimelech—his wife, Naomi,
and their two sons—appeared to be right in step with the "follow your
heart" philosophy, with disastrous results following their decision to
leave Bethlehem for Moab.

In addition to the historic enmity between Israel and Moab, the real
issue in Moab was the people's worship of false gods, notably Chemosh.
Moabites believed that fertility—in the field and the womb—was guaranteed by the sacrifice of their children. Pagan priests oversaw a hid-
eous ritual in which a firstborn child was killed in the fire of the god
Chemosh.

Jehovah God detested this practice and commanded his people in
Leviticus 18:21, "Do not give any of your children to be sacrificed to
[the gods]" (NIV). This was the culture, then, into which Elimelech and
Naomi chose to bring their family.

With this setting as the backdrop, if we could hear Naomi tell her
own story, it might sound something like this:

Elimelech and I watched as the rains diminished and the fields
around Bethlehem turned brown. Our herds began to shrink.
Everyone could see it: the region was heading for famine. Bethlehem, "the house of bread," was little more than a wasteland
when we decided to pack up our sons, say goodbye to family,
and hightail it out of there.

God had warned us in his Word: disobedience to his law
and consorting with idols would lead to dire consequences.
We just didn't believe him. We felt like we could decide what
was best for us and our family.

So instead of repenting, we ran. Life was never the same after that.

When we heard that just fifty miles east in Moab, food was plentiful and life was good, we headed for greener pastures. Except the grass didn't turn out to be greener.

True to his word, God allowed hard consequences from our decision to flee to Moab. All we found there was a dead end.

It started when my dear Elimelech passed away, leaving our two sons and me to survive far from our community of faith back in Israel. When my husband died, I thought I would die too. I see it now; this should have been my wake-up call: "Time to head home!" But instead of returning to Bethlehem, I stayed in Moab.

I knew about Jehovah's prohibition of his people intermarrying with pagan nations. But my sons, Mahlon and Chilion, were already of marrying age and the trip back to Israel was so long. Plus the boys had each fallen for two Moabites, Orpah and Ruth. We all needed a little happiness. Who was I to object?

They were good enough girls. And at first all seemed well. But after ten years of marriage (with no children born to either son), I knew we were in trouble.

Then things went from bad to worse. Both Mahlon and Chilion died in Moab. I felt like a cracked, empty water skin good for nothing but to be thrown on the fire.

Oh, those were hard days! Yet right in the middle of these harsh consequences, Jehovah invited me to do what Elimelech and I should have done years before in Israel: repent, return, and cry out to God for his mercy. He offered me something good and life-giving, a path back to his people and his blessings.

Instead of giving me further consequences for disobedience, he gave me an unexpected gift. He gave me Ruth.

When Mahlon and Chilion died, I told my daughters-in-law, "Go, return each of you to her mother's house. May the LORD deal kindly with you, as you have dealt with the dead and with me. The LORD grant that you may find rest, each of you in the house of her husband."

> **Jehovah invited me to do what Elimelech and I should have done years before in Israel: repent, return, and cry out to God for his mercy.**

Orpah finally agreed that she would be better off returning to her parents' household. But not Ruth. I will never forget the words she spoke to me—and kept every day thereafter: "Do not urge me to leave you or to return from following you. For where you go I will go, and where you lodge I will lodge. Your people shall be my people, and your God my God. Where you die I will die, and there will I be buried. May the LORD do so to me and more also if anything but death parts me from you."

As I heard these words come from a Moabite, I was cut to the quick. They revealed a heart in tune with Jehovah's own faithful love, his *hesed*. "I'm all in," Ruth said to me in those words. "I am parting forever from my people, my culture, and my god. And I am throwing my lot in completely with you, Naomi, and your god. Whatever happens to you will happen to me. I will be with you and for you—even to the end."

God finally got my attention. When all the other paths I chose turned out to be filled with roadblocks, God opened my eyes to see the one road that was always available—the road paved with humility headed back home.

Bolstered by Ruth's love, I felt ready to face the long trek back to Bethlehem. We had heard the famine was now over. Perhaps we would find shelter among my people there.

True to his word, from the moment I made the first move toward home, God began to bless us. We came to Bethlehem at the beginning of the barley harvest. Surely that was a good sign. But God had more than barley with which to fill us. He had a plan for us that involved marriage, children, grand-babies, and a future overflowing with promise.

When I returned to Bethlehem, the whole town was stirred. "Do you remember Naomi? Elimelech's wife? She's back, but without her husband or sons. She actually brought a Moabi-tess with her!" It was big news.

But I could see it in the women's eyes when they rushed to welcome us—the thinly veiled shock at my appearance. Some held back, barely recognizing me.

I told them, "Do not call me Naomi; call me Mara, for the Almighty has dealt very bitterly with me. I went away full, but the LORD has brought me back empty ... the LORD has testified against me and the Almighty has brought calamity upon me."

But God was at work for my good. It started when Ruth headed out to the fields that first day, empty-handed but de-termined to work. Through the Lord's guidance, she ended up gleaning grain in the field of a kinsman, Boaz. When she found favor in his sight and came home carrying a full ephah of bar-ley, I knew God had guided me to come back to my people.

WHAT'S A KINSMAN-REDEEMER?

In addition to being able to glean leftover grain from the edges of a field, as Ruth did in Boaz's fields, another benefit of being part of God's covenant community was the provision of a "kinsman-redeemer."[1]

In Hebrew the term for this person is *goel* and refers to a male relative who would act on behalf of a family member in dire need. The term is related to Old

Testament laws pertaining to land redemption. A kinsman-redeemer could buy back land sold by his relative in order to keep the land in the family (and continue the family's line). "Both the land law and levirate marriage were intended to preserve family and land—covenant matters of the first degree . . . social provisions by which God's covenant promises could continue to be realized even for *families in crisis*" (emphasis added).[2]

When Naomi returned to Bethlehem, she moved back into proximity of all the blessing and provision of God: his promises to bless obedience, the ability to glean in the fields, and the possibility of help from a kinsman-redeemer. Ruth 3 opens with Naomi broaching the subject of marriage with her daughter-in-law. No doubt these women were hoping for a kinsman-redeemer who might buy Elimelech's land and marry his closest marriageable female relative (Ruth) in an attempt to continue the family name.

I can see it now. The two women concocting Ruth's Match.com profile, which might have read something like this: "Single Moabite widow seeks wealthy Israelite landowner with a good heart to share life and quiet nights by the fire. Must want children."

Ruth's profile wasn't needed, of course, because God was already at work, leading her to glean in the fields of Boaz—who "just happened" to be a family relation who could take on the kinsman-redeemer role.

Having heard Ruth's account of meeting with Boaz, I knew this was a match worth making. We prepared Ruth for a night on the threshing floor and a possible encounter with Boaz. All went according to plan.

When Ruth returned the next morning, she told me that she had followed my instructions. She waited until Boaz finished eating and drinking and had fallen asleep. Then she uncovered his feet. When Boaz awakened to cover his cold feet, Ruth revealed her identity and asked him to fulfill the role of kinsman-redeemer: "I am Ruth, your servant. Spread your wings over your servant, for you are a redeemer." Okay, so it wasn't exactly a romantic proposal, but it got the job done.

True to his word, the next morning Boaz took up my case at the city gate. He spoke to the kinsman who was first in line to buy the family's land, marry Ruth, and attempt to build back the house of Elimelech. That man was interested in the land, but not in Ruth, so he urged Boaz to take his right of redemption.

And that was exactly what Boaz did. All the people at the gate that day bore witness to this significant transaction. More than that, they pronounced a blessing on Boaz and Ruth's union, asking God to multiply their offspring.

And God answered their prayer with abundant blessing. In a happy ending no one saw coming, Boaz married Ruth and she conceived a son. Imagine our joy when Ruth came to give me the news! A child meant joy, prosperity, and continuity of the family. It meant provision and comfort in my old age.

The news was so wonderful that the women of my faith community gathered to bless me. In their words I heard echoes of God's joyful voice as well: "Blessed be the LORD, who has not left you this day without a redeemer, and may his name be renowned in Israel! He shall be to you a restorer of life and a nourisher of your old age."

And so it was. I took little Obed and laid him on my lap and became his nurse. All those past losses, the deaths of my husband and sons, were now redeemed in the gift of my grandson. God had led us back to where we belonged—at home with him and his people.

Return to the Faith Community

Naomi's story was filled with crises. Some, like the deaths of her husband and sons, were tragedies she couldn't prevent. Others—like facing widowhood and destitution in a foreign land—arose from her choice to leave her faith community. And as the weight of her losses grew, she became "Mara"—bitter.

Sister, can you relate? Have your own losses left you feeling hopeless? Maybe you, too, have been wandering away from God's people and grown comfortable in the company of bitterness. Maybe like Naomi you wonder how your losses could possibly be redeemed.

Just as the Baileys enfolded my siblings and me after our mother's devastating accident, God used the covenant community to care for Ruth and Naomi. God's people effectively "sheltered them from the elements" of widowhood, poverty, and extreme vulnerability. What is the modern equivalent of this remarkable, life-giving community? Sister, it's the church, the body of Christ, God's provision for our growth and care.

Isolation from God's people didn't work so well for Naomi and Elimelech, and it doesn't work well for us either. The church is God's provision for our growth, and we cannot live abundantly without it.

A global pandemic interrupted in-person worship for many. Statistics from Barna tell us one-third of church-goers never returned to church.[3] Perhaps you and your family are included in that statistic. But a steady diet of Zoom church, sermon podcasts, or worshiping by yourself won't lead to deeper union with Christ.

More often it leads to isolation, self-appointed authority, and stunted growth—if any growth at all. There are no lone rangers in the body of Christ. We will never grow into the likeness of Christ (Ephesians 4:11–16) or fulfill God's will for our lives apart from our brothers and sisters in Christ in a local congregation. If you are not a committed part of a local church, God may be calling you to seek one—or return to the one you have left.

Naomi's story reminds me not only of my own but of my mother's. I remember her beauty, her intelligence, her ability to attract male attention. She had all the gifts the world values, but my mother would admit today that before the accident she was living on her own terms, not God's.

On the night of the accident that took her leg, she suffered an incalculable loss, the effects of which she and our family still feel keenly. But decades later, my mother is not the same person. She is a new creation. God has truly fulfilled the promise of Romans 8:28 to us. The loss of my mother's leg (and mobility) ultimately brought her to the end of herself and to a place more firmly rooted in God and his people. She truly "came home." She learned to lean deeply on Jesus as her Kinsman-Redeemer. Beautiful, lasting fruit has been the result.

The crisis of my mother's accident and resulting disability became an unexpected portal through which she passed (over many years) from trusting in her giftedness to resting in God's sacred refuge for her in Jesus, her Kinsman-Redeemer.

Sheltered by Jesus, Our Kinsman-Redeemer

Far from a formulaic Hollywood romance, the love and commitment between Ruth and Boaz is rare and beautiful. If the narrative stopped there, we would have simply enjoyed an ancient love story. But there is so much more that God would have us discover in the book of Ruth. As Bible scholar Iain Duguid says, "What Naomi and Ruth most needed was not simply a redeemer to rescue them from their earthly poverty and danger, nor even a husband for Ruth. Rather, they needed a heavenly Redeemer to rescue them from their sin."[4]

In the story of Ruth and Boaz, God would have us discern a far greater love story. It's *your* love story, sister. And it is found in the arms of your Kinsman-Redeemer, Jesus Christ.

Perhaps like Ruth, you are the outsider who grew up on the wrong side of the tracks. It feels like you have never been able to catch a break. Life has always been an uphill climb. Or maybe you're a Naomi, struggling with deep losses and feeling far from home. But what if, through one crisis after another, God is inviting you into a completely new life?

TRANSFORMING TRUTH

When losses taunt you with the lie, "God's abandoned you. You are on your own," let the promise of your Kinsman-Redeemer encourage your heart: "Beloved, even when you were in your far country, I loved and pursued you. It's time to come home to fullness: your inheritance among my people and the shelter of my arms."

Safe Beneath His Wings

Ruth had her kinsman-redeemer, and you have one too. As good and faithful a man as Boaz was, he was a mere foreshadowing of Jesus Christ, who in a far more dramatic way perfectly rescued us and brought us back to abundant life in the Father.

Do you remember how Boaz blessed Ruth for her faithfulness? He said, "The LORD repay you for what you have done, and a full reward be given you by the LORD, the God of Israel, under whose wings you have come to take refuge!" (Ruth 2:12). On the night when Ruth visited Boaz on the threshing floor, she asked him to "spread your wings over your servant, for you are a redeemer" (3:9).

Here Ruth and Boaz point to a beautiful image—found throughout Scripture—of God protecting his people under the refuge of his wings. As Boaz covered Ruth, he was also pointing to Jesus, who "shall rise with healing in [his] wings" (Malachi 4:2) and who in Luke 13:34 longed to cover the inhabitants of Jerusalem: "How often would I have gathered your children together as a hen gathers her brood under her wings, and you were not willing!"

The Old Testament gives us a picture of God as the faithful husband of an unfaithful people.[5] The New Testament deepens this marriage imagery in depicting Jesus as the Bridegroom who pays the ultimate bride price—ransoming his bride, the church, through his blood shed on the cross. Sent by the Father to redeem you, Jesus came to give you a new life by uniting himself to you forever.

If you have never done so before, will you receive Jesus Christ's proposal, his offer to be *your* redeemer? Or perhaps you've already accepted Christ as your Bridegroom, but you are being called to "renew your vows" and return to his embrace. How he longs to "spread the wings" of his garment over you, sister.

A Sacred Romance

Jesus offers you a love story every bit as beautiful as Ruth's. Consider the many ways Jesus serves as your Kinsman-Redeemer:

- *Jesus shelters you with his righteousness.* Just as Boaz covered Ruth with his robe, symbolically protecting her from need, loneliness, and an uncertain future, so Jesus shelters you with his robe of righteousness (Isaiah 61:10).
- *Jesus is your nearest of kin.* As God with flesh on, Jesus is your nearest of kin, who is powerfully able to sympathize with you, having been tempted in every way as we are but without sin (Hebrews 4:14–16). He gets us.
- *Jesus is your provider.* More than just physical provision, Jesus gives you what your heart most longs for: fullness. You are made for abundant life that is only found in him (John 10:10). When you have fallen for the world's "philosophy and empty deceit," you can turn to Jesus and be "filled in him" (Colossians 2:10).
- *Jesus produces fruit from your union.* As your Kinsman-Redeemer, Jesus shares his very life with you. His Spirit fills you and produces beautiful, long-term fruit: love, joy, peace, patience, kindness, goodness, faithfulness, gentleness, and self-control (Galatians 5:22–23).
- *Jesus keeps covenant with God on your behalf.* Jesus Christ, the sinless god-man, perfectly keeps the covenant—which we fail to keep—*for us* (Hebrews 8:8). Just as Boaz stood up for Naomi and Ruth at the city gate, Jesus stands up for you. He faithfully claims you. He buys you back. You are his. And no one can undo what he has accomplished on your behalf.

- *Jesus redeems your inheritance.* When you had lost your inheritance through sin, when your life was unfruitful in the arms of other lovers, Jesus took you back fully to himself. Boaz paid full price to redeem the land owned by Elimelech, but Jesus paid a price far costlier than that to redeem you (Hebrews 9:15).
- *Jesus is your heavenly husband.* Jesus cares for you, provides for you, and serves you. As the perfect husband, he loves you unconditionally and serves you sacrificially. He faithfully protects you and provides for you (Ephesians 5:25–27).

Trusting Jesus as Your Kinsman-Redeemer

Perhaps like Naomi, you have left the community of faith for your own version of Moab. You have pursued what looked like greener pastures through a life on your own terms, apart from God and the faith community. What "other lovers" have you thought would cover and protect you? Was it the desire for perfect fulfillment in a grand romance? In career success? In financial security? In pursuit of "the good life"? Have you sought false shelter in Moab (following your own path outside the church) but want to return home to the house of faith?

Beloved, Jesus longs for your return. He is your perfect heavenly husband who will never leave nor forsake you. God says to you: "I have loved you with an everlasting love; therefore with lovingkindness I have drawn you" (Jeremiah 31:3 NKJV). His word is completely trustworthy because it is rooted in his perfect, unchanging character.

Sister, every loss you have experienced, every relational betrayal, every heartbreak you carry from human relationships can be healed in the love of your Kinsman-Redeemer. He is the answer to your heart's hunger for fullness—for shelter, belonging, and joy. Do you long for the faithful loving-kindness (*hesed*) Ruth experienced? It is yours in a relationship with Jesus, your Kinsman-Redeemer.

Enter the Sacred Refuge
of Jesus, Your Kinsman-Redeemer

Jesus may be saying something like this to you:

I saw you, beloved, when you set out on the road to Moab. You packed your bags and didn't look back. How it broke my heart.

Not trusting me to meet your needs opened the door to distraction. When it had done its dirty work, gradually, imperceptibly, your heart cooled toward me. You pined after the fullness you thought you would find in Moab: Independence. Happiness. Meaning. Prosperity. But you have discovered they are poor substitutes for me and what I alone can give.

I know what crisis you are suffering through right now, in your far country. Life in Moab has emptied you out. It has left you "wretched, pitiable, poor, blind, and naked." How I long to see you turn around, see my love for you, and begin the trek back to me. For having provided your pardon, I wait here with open arms for you to come home. I am waiting for you, beloved.

I know you long to be fulfilled in a relationship with someone who sees who you really are, knows you better than you know yourself, and loves you with a sacrificial love. I am that One.

Even now I am standing up for you as your Kinsman and Redeemer. I would take your part, advocate for you. I long to spread the corner of my garment over you, to cover your nakedness with my own righteousness. I long to unite myself to you and pour my life into you. I long to give you a hope-filled future and a rich legacy.

All the fullness of God dwells in me, and I have given you fullness in union with myself. I am committed to you, beloved. You can trust me, dear one. My love is with you and for you.

Won't you take that first step back to me?[6]

REST Under His Wings

Breathe deeply as you quiet yourself in God's presence.

Release control.
1. Consider some of the losses you have sustained: Have they caused you to doubt God's goodness or trustworthiness?
2. In what ways have you not trusted that God has the power to save you—not only from sin, but from loneliness, from every kind of hunger, and from loss?

Father, you know my past losses. Please draw near to me by your Holy Spirit and lead me out of hiding in the areas where I struggle to trust you. I recognize that I am not in control of my life, including its losses or gains. You are. Help me to let go of any bitterness or doubt that has made me wander from you. I give you my heart and trust you with my future.

Exchange your *loss* for the love of your *Kinsman-Redeemer* and his people.
3. Has the heartache of your past losses caused you to isolate yourself from God or others? What has this cost you?
4. How might God use your heart hunger resulting from past losses to draw you to himself and/or his people? Write a prayer about this to your loving Kinsman-Redeemer.

Lord, some of my losses cost me so much that I vowed never to let anyone hurt me that way again. Please draw me out of hiding in the dark into your light and presence. Help me to trust that you are my one safe place.

See yourself in union with Christ.

5. What aspects of Jesus as a Kinsman-Redeemer do you most need to experience in your life right now? Ask God to help you remember these truths and live in light of your union with Jesus.

Father, help me to live out the implications of Jesus's faithful work of redeeming my life. Remind me—in the context of your people, the local church—that I am part of your covenant community. Help me trust myself and my heart to those who bear your name.

Trust Christ as your Kinsman-Redeemer.

6. Create a breath prayer that reflects your longing for fullness with God as your Kinsman-Redeemer. (Examples: "Lord . . . I am coming home to you." "Jesus . . . draw me close." "Jesus, I give you my losses. . . . Jesus, give me your fullness.") Turn to this prayer throughout your day as a reminder to trust in him.

CHAPTER 8

Comforted

Finding Shelter in Christ's Compassion

Trust in him at all times, O people;
pour out your heart before him;
God is a refuge for us.
—PSALM 62:8

When my heart is broken in disappointment, can I still trust God?

TWO YEARS AGO my friend Katrina and her husband, John, received a disturbing phone call one morning from their daughter-in-law Jenna. "Charles was supposed to be home from work hours ago," the quavering voice said. "He's not answering his phone, and I don't know what to do."

Katrina and John began calling the police and local hospitals but learned nothing. They packed a bag and prayed all the way to their son's home seven hours away.

The couple processed various theories together, but not the one they feared most. Charles had grown up with a strong faith, but in recent years there had been less evidence of his walk with God. They had been praying fervently for Charles to come back to the Lord and live powerfully for him. Now as they drove, they prayed for answers, for wisdom, and for Charles's protection.

During the drive, John had a nudge in his spirit, an impression from the Holy Spirit: *He is home.* They hoped this meant that Charles was heading home.

John and Katrina were in conversation throughout the day with the police during the trip. As the day progressed, their fears began to grow despite the hint of reassurance that Charles was home.

That night when they pulled into the apartment complex where Charles and Jenna lived, they saw police officers lining the walkway. The news hit them with brute force. Their son had been killed by a drunk driver as he walked home from work the night before.

It's what those of us with children or grandchildren dread. A moment of feeling like our heart is being ripped out of our chest. A pain that sends us spinning into paroxysms of grief and threatens to undo us.

The family's only consolation was hearing from the police that Charles had died instantly and not suffered.

What is truly amazing was how God showed up to comfort John and Katrina in the days that followed. He did so with his Word, in the prayers of others on their behalf, and in the love they received from their local church. But God did even more. The next day, they received calls and texts from three close friends and family members saying they had heard the same message from the Lord that John had: "He is home."

This message became a balm to their excruciating pain, removing death's sting. Their confidence grew that Charles had indeed made it home and into his Savior's arms.

Katrina later told me, "Charles was set free from chronic pain. He escaped the problems in this world and experienced what it was like to enter the presence of the Lord in eternity."

Two days after the loss of her son, she wrote this in her journal:

> Lord, I know You love us and are in control. Thank You for telling us that Charles is home. He is now free from pain. I ask you to be with Jenna. This loss is so difficult for us. It may even be harder for her. Please show me how to support her through this.[1]

Sheltered in Love

I can't speak for you, but I know I wouldn't have been where Katrina was so soon after this life-altering loss. What was at work here? Are John and Katrina super saints who float through life four inches above the ground? They would say a resounding "No."

The only explanation is that Katrina and John were supernaturally sheltered by their loving Father. He hemmed them in and held them as no one else could in the sacred refuge Jesus built for them and their son.

Sister, what has put you in darkness? What (or who) has died and made you feel as though a part of you is gone as well? Is it a husband, child, or friend whose absence you constantly feel? Is it your dreams for children and grandchildren? A thriving career or business you built—and lost? Or is it a growing malaise about the state of our culture and world and deep concern about what the next generation will inherit?

When we sit in this place of despair and hopelessness, we desperately need to know we are not alone. We also need to know there is hope that things can change.

Of course, none of us would choose to place ourselves in heartbreaking circumstances. But often, it's in the severe moments of life where we most profoundly experience God's mercy and compassion. God may be asking you, "What if your heartbreak is a portal that will lead you into the safe place under my wings?"

Mary of Bethany's Story

I'm a big fan of Mary of Bethany—she's my girl! Every time we meet her in Scripture, she is at the feet of Jesus. What a perfect posture in which to experience his sacred refuge.

Perhaps, like Mary, you have learned to respond to Jesus's invitation to sit at his feet (Luke 10:39). In that place you have been discovering who he is. You know that Jesus is powerful, good, and merciful. When you have a need, you cry out to him. And you have sometimes seen him answer decisively and quickly. But this sacred sister's story has even more to teach us.

Mary of Bethany's experience sheds light into our dark times. Like when we cry out for help, but God *doesn't* do what we ask of him. What about when the crisis gets worse and we have no sense of where he is and what he's doing. Or when the person or relationship most dear to us is on the line and we watch it sift through our fingers like sand.

When life gets messy or downright broken, can you still believe that Jesus is powerful, good, and merciful, as Katrina did even after the loss of her son? Jesus sheltered Mary of Bethany in his presence and with his love. But after her brother Lazarus died, she asked the same questions you may be wrestling with: "Jesus isn't who I thought he was. Does he still love me? When my heart is broken in disappointment, can I still trust God?"

For answers to these questions, let's enter Mary's story in John 11:1–44, which reveals the character, power, and compassion of Jesus Christ when life falls apart.

The setting? A town called Bethany, just two miles east of Jerusalem. It was nearing the end of Jesus's public ministry, and the religious leaders of the day were looking for any excuse to do away with him. The situation? A family dear to Jesus, in whose home he often stayed when coming into or out of Jerusalem, was in trouble. Jesus was away on the far side of the Jordan River. Lazarus, the beloved brother of Mary and Martha of Bethany, was gravely ill.

WHERE IS JESUS?

Word reached Jesus that Lazarus was sick. Now, don't miss this important detail John included in verses 5–6: "Now Jesus loved Martha and her sister and Lazarus. So, when he heard that Lazarus was ill, he stayed two days longer in the place where he was."

"Wait a minute!" we want to cry out. "Jesus, if you loved them, why wouldn't you make haste to swoop in and save the day? Or couldn't you have simply said the word and healed Lazarus from a distance, as you did on other occasions?" (see Luke 7:1–10).

Clearly, there was something going on here that this family—and we—couldn't yet understand.

Don't miss this crucial truth: What happened to Lazarus's family did not mean Jesus had removed his love. He loved them *in* this tragedy. His love is constant regardless of circumstance. He does not change even when our situations do.

But God's loving us does not mean we are shielded from the consequences of living in a broken world. We will experience the darkness of the "India ink" of sin, disappointment, betrayal, and heartache. The difference between those in Christ and those living on their own is that when crisis hits us, we have someone who is right there with us, surrounding us with comfort.

Those who do not yet trust this truth suffer alone and without hope.

Those in Christ know that there is a "why" behind our pain, even if we can't understand it now. Something is happening that will ultimately be to the glory of God. Jesus may not always do exactly what we expect or comprehend, but he's always present—wrapping us in his love.

With this as our backdrop, I imagine that if we could hear Mary of Bethany tell her story, it would sound something like this:

When we first saw our dear Lazarus languishing, Martha and I locked eyes over his bed in deep concern. Moments later, Martha had the solution.

"We will call the Teacher. How many times have we seen him heal the sick? He loves Lazarus like his own brother. He will come." Knowing my tender heart, she looked me in the eyes and pronounced, "All will be well, Mary."

So that very day we sent a message to Jesus who was across the Jordan with his disciples: "Lord, he whom you love is ill."

Had our home not become Jesus's home when he was near Jerusalem? Was not our family his adopted family? Even though there was a mounting threat from the religious leaders, we knew Jesus would come.

Anticipating his arrival, early on the second day, we hired a boy from Bethany to stand watch and let us know the moment he saw Jesus heading our way.

Day two came and went. Lazarus's condition worsened.

"Surely he will come today," we told one another.

But he did not.

On the morning of the third day, I myself walked out to the road to watch for Jesus. There was no sign of him. And no word had come back through the messenger.

By the following day, even Martha was worried. Lazarus was now so far gone, he was not aware of what was happening.

That night we watched as our beloved brother's life ebbed away. A faint heartbeat. Fainter. And then he was gone.

I could not help myself. I howled with grief when we knew it was too late to save Lazarus. He was dead. And no help from Jesus. I thought my heart would break in two.

Martha and I had lost our brother and, with his death, any sense of normal life. How we missed his laugh echoing through the house, his silly jokes cracked at our expense.

But we had lost even more than his company. Since the death of our parents, Lazarus had been the source of our social standing and financial stability. With his passing, and Martha and I unmarried, we were facing a life of poverty and want.

But it was even more than that. As keenly as I missed my dear Lazarus, Jesus's absence created an acute ache inside. No man or Rabbi had ever invited women to sit at his feet. But Jesus did. Since he had invited me to join his circle of followers, I had come to love Jesus with everything in me. He had become my heart's chief delight.

Jesus didn't come when we called for him. What did it mean? No one knew me as he did—and still loved me, I knew, with a fierce affection. Jesus's not coming in time to save Lazarus planted a seed of doubt in me about his love. My heart

cried out, "I thought I knew who Jesus was. Ultimate goodness. Unlimited power. Deep compassion. Now I am not so
sure."

I'll admit it. The weight of both losses put me in a dark
place. All I wanted to do was hide in the house with the
mourners who had come from Jerusalem.

Then we got word that Jesus had finally come. Martha ran
to meet him outside the village. I couldn't make myself move.
Sadness, anger, and confusion rooted me in place as I lamented
with the mourners.

Martha came back to our house after meeting with Jesus.
She approached me gently. Taking my arm and leading me to
a quiet corner, she told me, "The Teacher is here, and he is
asking for you."

The Teacher, asking for me?

My pain cried out, "He's come too late. I don't want to see
him. Why would I trust him again?" But memories of being with Jesus, listening to him, and being accepted by him
flooded my mind.

Something deep within me shifted. I rose up and ran to him
outside the village. I needed to see him, to ask him why he
hadn't come. I needed to understand. On the way, I rehearsed
all my questions.

But the moment I saw Jesus standing there, I could do nothing but fall at his feet. His beautiful feet, which carried this
teacher and prophet to do God's will and proclaim good news.
Those blessed feet where I had sat many times to listen and
learn and love.

Sobbing, I tried to give words to what was exploding from
my heart: "Lord, if you had been here, my brother would not
have died." The mourners who had followed me from the
house murmured in agreement.

And then I perceived a strange sound coming from Jesus.

It was a cry such as I had never heard from any man. Starting as a low growl, it crescendoed with such force that I cowered before him. "Aagggghhhhh!" It sounded like the roar of a lion. Anger. Sadness. Frustration. His exclamation seemed to say, "It didn't have to be this way!" Still clinging to his feet, I felt Jesus's body shake as sobs erupted throughout his frame.

Then this unforeseen truth hit me with full force: Jesus had not tarried because of indifference to our suffering. In this moment, he was entering fully into our loss and grief. Jesus's spirit was deeply moved and troubled—as ours were.

> **Jesus had not tarried because of indifference to our suffering. In this moment, he was entering fully into our loss and grief.**

We felt a shift. It was as if all the emotion Jesus had expressed became an urgent need to act. He asked us, "Where have you laid him?"

Did Jesus just want to be closer to Lazarus and grieve there? No. Something else was happening. I got up and joined Martha, leading Jesus to the tomb. It was a cave, sealed by a large stone that required four men to roll it into place.

Martha, ever practical, reminded Jesus of the foul odor that was sure to be present in the grave. But Jesus asked her, "Did I not tell you that if you believed you would see the glory of God?"

No one would see anything unless the stone was taken away, so Martha and I gave the command to do it and clutched each other. Even as the stench from Lazarus's tomb wafted past us, we knew something extraordinary was happening.

Jesus lifted his eyes to heaven and prayed, "Father, I thank you that you have heard me. I knew that you always hear me, but I said this on account of the people standing around, that they may believe that you sent me."

Then Jesus shouted toward the open tomb, his voice full of authority and confidence: "Lazarus! Come out!"

I'll be honest. At that moment Martha and I were caught, like many of the onlookers, somewhere between embarrassment, disbelief, and flickering hope. Jesus had commanded the impossible. I wondered, *Does Jesus really have power over life and death?*

We waited. And held our breath. Someone in the crowd coughed.

At first there was nothing, just the black maw of the open grave and the reek of rotting flesh.

Then we discerned a shuffling noise. We made out movement coming forth from the murky darkness.

Our hearts lurched. Martha rushed forward to get a closer look.

But when we saw the familiar form of our brother emerging from the darkness, the grave clothes tightly wrapped around his hands and feet and face, we both leapt toward him.

The moments afterward were a maelstrom of emotions. Euphoric joy. Shock and awe. Complete amazement.

Jesus commanded, "Unbind him and let him go." And so we did.

A week later, as Jesus's time was coming to an end, Martha and I threw a dinner party for him and his followers.

Preparing for the evening, I found myself reflecting on all that had happened. Martha and I had asked Jesus to come and heal our brother. Had he come when we wanted and kept Lazarus from dying, we never would have experienced the shelter that surrounded us in Jesus's compassion. We never would have known him as our resurrection and life.

Jesus Weeps with You

I wonder, dear sister, what crisis are you currently facing? What death scenario are you walking through? And what have you asked God to do in the midst of it?

Is it a prodigal child or grandchild you long to see restored? A tangled relationship that desperately needs healing? Maybe you've been praying for answers and miracles that you have yet to see. Have you been tempted, like Mary, to hide from God in heartbreak and disappointment? Or maybe, like Martha, you're feeling God is somehow unfair because your expectations have not been met?

Maybe, like both women, you believe God is powerful, but when the weight of the crisis is intense, you doubt his goodness. What if God is doing something far greater than you can imagine? What if this crisis is his invitation for you to encounter him in a deeper and greater way?

In Mary's story, as it's related in John 11:34, Jesus asked the sisters where they had laid Lazarus. And then verse 35 tells us, simply, "Jesus wept." The Logos, the Bright and Morning Star, the Prince of Peace, and the Rock of our Salvation shed salty tears.

This is the only time this word *wept* is used in the New Testament. Jesus loved Mary, and seeing her tears moved him to tears. He is similarly moved by your suffering, sister. Dane Ortlund observes in his book *Gentle and Lowly*, "What was his deepest anguish? The anguish of others. What drew his heart out to the point of tears? The tears of others."[2]

Do you see Jesus here, the "man of sorrows and acquainted with grief" (Isaiah 53:3)? Jesus knew exactly what he was about to do, yet he entered fully into the sorrow of Lazarus's death. Sister, he weeps with those who weep.

TRANSFORMING TRUTH

In your deepest pain, heartbreak says, "You're on your own. Why would you trust God, who allowed this loss, to help you bear it?" Instead, tune in to the voice who calls to you in compassion, "Beloved, I dwell in the midst of brokenness. I am here, with you at this moment, to carry and comfort you through this pain."

In your pain and disappointment, let this image be seared in your mind. Then let it silence once and for all the enemy's lie that in the crisis you are currently walking through, God is somehow far off and unaffected by your suffering.

Would a distant God create the world, watch it fall, and then promise as early as Genesis 3:15 (and throughout the entire Old Testament) that the Messiah would come and deal with sin and death once and for all? Would a dispassionate God send his Son to die an excruciating death upon a Roman cross, experiencing rejection in our place, so the Father would never turn his face away from us?

No, this is a God who comes near and shelters us in our worst moments. Like Mary, we can fall weeping at Jesus's feet, pouring out our sorrows, and know he weeps with us. Each tear we shed is precious to him. Psalm 56:8 tells us God puts them in his bottle, notes each in his book.

Sister, your heart may be breaking, but it is not breaking alone—Jesus is never unaffected by your pain. You don't need to censor your heartache or anger with him; your messy feelings will not make him walk away. You may not have the answers and explanations you want, but one thing you can always be sure of—Jesus weeps right beside you and holds you in your pain.

Sheltered by Jesus's Compassion

Mary of Bethany's story provides a moving picture of Jesus's compassion. And that same compassion will be there for each of us whenever life sends us sad and overwhelming circumstances.

Yet so often, our enemy lures us away from Jesus by shooting arrows of doubt at our hearts. As Mary can attest, confusion and seemingly unanswered prayers can make us feel like hiding away from Jesus's tender compassion at the very moments we most need to lean into it. And even when we do notice the reality of Jesus weeping beside us, it may not always feel like enough. What good are the tears, we might wonder, if all our hopes and dreams remain dead?

Thankfully, Jesus's compassion comes with his tears *and* his power to heal. It's a comfort that not only gives us his presence but also starts to piece our broken hearts back together. As it did for John and Katrina, it is a hope that breathes resurrection life back into our spirits.

Sheltered by the Resurrection and the Life

In the background of Mary's story, her sister, Martha, dealt with the grief of Lazarus's death as well. Four days after they'd sent for him, Jesus returned to Bethany, and Martha ran to the outskirts of the village to meet him. Hurt and confused, she confronted Jesus with the obvious: "Lord, if you had been here, my brother would not have died." Then she added this powerful, faith-packed statement: "But even now I know that whatever you ask from God, God will give you" (John 11:21–22).

Jesus held out the promise that Lazarus "will rise again." Martha said, "I know that he will rise again in the resurrection on the last day" (vv. 23–24).

And that's when Jesus changed everything with this astonishing statement of his identity: "I am the resurrection and the life. Whoever believes in me, though he die, yet shall he live, and everyone who lives and believes in me shall never die. Do you believe this?" (vv. 25–26).

It's as if Jesus said, "You're thinking about something far off and remote, Martha. But I have come to earth, into your lives, and back to Bethany today to display my true identity as the source of life and resurrection power!" Bible scholar William Hendriksen says, "Jesus is the resurrection and the life in person, the full, blessed life of God. . . . He is the cause, source, and foundation of the believers' glorious resurrection. . . . With him removed, nothing but death is left. With him present, resurrection and life is assured."[3]

Martha, who had come a long way from her "harried hostess" days in Luke 10, then made one of the most magnificent faith proclamations in the New Testament. Filled with insight from the Holy Spirit, she cried out, "Yes, Lord; I believe that you are the Christ, the Son of God, who is coming into the world" (v. 27).

Martha identified Jesus as the Promised One. But in verses 25–26 Jesus announced a powerful aspect of his work as Messiah: in him the dead live and the living never die. Jesus was not just a life-giver to Lazarus, who was dead; he was a life-giver to Martha, who was still living! What Martha wished Jesus had done for Lazarus, Jesus does for all those who come to him. He comes to bring life!

With his declaration, "I am the resurrection and the life," Jesus's words brought comfort to Martha. That same truth carried my friends Katrina and John through the loss of their son. How can these words comfort us today? How can this truth resurrect our personal circumstances?

Hendriksen unpacks the implications of Jesus's extraordinary statement: "What Martha scarcely dared to hope was about to become *real*, for he, who was the Prince of life *also at this moment*, was victor over death, over death in every form."[4]

In our moments of deepest grief and loss, our hearts may feel completely dead. But in his compassion, Jesus weeps with us and then comforts us with this truth: he is the one who brings dead things back to life. Jesus proved this when he resurrected Lazarus. He will prove it again when Katrina and John are reunited with their son in heaven, who made it home before they did.

Do You Believe This?

But what about in the meantime, you ask? How do I experience resurrection life in my crisis right now? When we experience heart-wrenching losses, we can choose to respond in destructive ways, such as numbing our pain with addictive behaviors. Or we can respond in a life-giving way by trusting that Jesus's love and presence are with us.

> ## Jesus weeps with us and then comforts us with this truth: he is the one who brings dead things back to life.

The most powerful response is to live on the strong, unshakable foundation of the gospel. The resurrection and the life Jesus offered Martha and Mary can also become ours when we trust that he reconciles us to the Father. He turns to each of us in our own times of struggle to ask us the same question he directed to Martha: "Do you believe this?" (John 11:26). Our answer will determine whether we stay in hiding or, like Mary when she heard Jesus was asking for her, choose to abide near him even before he answers our prayer.

Perhaps the crisis you are in feels like a death has taken place. It might be the death of a relationship, of a dream, or of peace and predictability. You wonder how you can experience Jesus as your "resurrection and life" when someone you love dearly has died or is ill.

That was the experience of my friend Nancy, who lost her husband just weeks before the pandemic began. A few years later, her daughter Carrie started to have unexplainable symptoms. She went to a small regional hospital that just "happened" to have a traveling endocrine specialist on board that week. That physician came to my friend and her daughter to break the news: "I'm afraid you have non-Hodgkin's large B-cell lymphoma. You are not going home. We need to treat this aggressive cancer immediately."

Soon Carrie was deep into chemo and suffering side effects. She woke my friend Nancy early one morning and said, "Mom, I'm in terrible pain. We have to go to the hospital."

Nancy shared with me what it was like to walk into the hospital where she had lost her mother, her husband, and now feared losing her daughter. Had God abandoned her in this new crisis?

> As we walked into that place of deep loss, I thought, *I can't do this again. I cannot lose another loved one.* Corrosive fear swept over me in waves. I started sweating profusely and experiencing severe heart palpitations.
>
> At that moment, I was stripped bare of any props or personal power. All I had was my relationship with the Lord. It was time to relinquish control of my daughter's situation and entrust her life into God's care.
>
> The Lord said to me, "This is exactly where I want you. I'm inviting you to rely on me in this situation. Will you trust me?"
>
> I did. In that moment, God brought me to the end of myself and I let go. He gave me grace to trust him, *even if* I didn't receive the outcome I longed for. That was the beginning of learning more about God's power and faithful love.
>
> I still had concerns afterward, but they were no longer based in fear. I went from being absolutely terrified to discovering that all I had to do was let the Lord have the situation. It was a hard journey to get to that point, but God didn't give up. He doesn't give up on us.[5]

Perhaps you can relate to Nancy's story. I can. There have been times (such as the loss of two babies to miscarriage) when I was tempted to react to loss like Mary, hiding from Jesus and others. I nursed my pain with thoughts of, *Jesus, I thought I knew you. I thought you were able to . . . Why didn't you show up when I called?*

And then I have heard a voice nearby speaking to me in my heartbreak: "The Teacher is here and is calling for you" (John 11:28). He calls me out from a place of hiding. Of lowering my expectations. Of sleepwalking through my life. Of numbing the pain through escapism.

As I come to him, pouring out my tears and questions, he helps me roll away the stones that have kept me from seeing his resurrection power: distraction, fear, idolatry, selfishness, unbelief.

Then he says to me, "Dear one, you have only begun to know me . . . I am far more powerful, more loving, and more wise than you have begun to imagine."

Enter the Sacred Refuge of Jesus's Compassion

Perhaps Jesus would say something like this to you today:

> Beloved, I know what death scenarios you are walking through right now. I know how they make you feel—like you are sitting alone in a cave, waiting for light and hope to come. I know you have cried out to me but have not yet received the answer your heart sought, or in the time you expected. I know you are disappointed. I know that you asked. Sought. Knocked. With apparently no answer.
>
> Do not give up, beloved. I am so much more than you thought I was.
>
> Dear one, I have some hard questions for you: What has been sitting in the tomb of your spirit, rotting in the dark? What have you given up on, and why? What has the enemy told you is dead and gone, never to be resurrected? Has he convinced you to lower your expectations and just settle, to give up and not risk disappointment again? What stones have been rolled across this tomb, locking you in the dark, hopeless? Are you ready to see those stones rolled away once and for all?
>
> Know that I am the Resurrection and the Life. I did not go to the cross in your place and die your death so that you would live life in the shadows. I came to give you life, and that abundantly. I came to earth and put on flesh to understand your suffering firsthand. To be able to enter into your heartbreak with complete understanding and compassion. I sent my Holy Spirit to be near you, in you, in order to comfort you, dear one.

Perhaps you have begun to assume that I am not good and not to be trusted. I invite you to consider the possibility that I am far bigger, far more loving, and more powerful than you have even dared to imagine. In this time of waiting in the middle of heartache, know that I am revealing myself to you in a way that you would not have seen or understood without the crisis you are currently facing.

For as heavy as your burden is right now, it will one day seem light and momentary.

What if you do not need to see the outcome you long for to experience me as the Resurrection and the Life? Beloved, can you trust me, even if you do not see the glory of God through this loss during your lifetime? The day will come when I wipe away every tear from your eyes as I restore what's been lost. But resurrection life begins now, in the new life I have planted in you by my Holy Spirit, and as I teach you to trust in my plan and power, *even if* you don't yet understand it.

If you are ready for renewal, then you have already begun experiencing me as the Resurrection and the Life.

I call you to come out! Beloved, come forth now from a place of darkness and hopelessness and, like Lazarus, gulp in the new life that my Holy Spirit now breathes into you! Come to me, my sister, my bride. I have come to comfort you in my presence.[6]

REST Under His Wings

Spend time quieting yourself in God's presence.

Release control.

1. Consider the ways that you have been hiding from God in heartbreak. Have you turned to false shelters (numbing behaviors, lowering expectations, etc.) to handle your pain?
2. In what ways have you struggled to trust God through difficult

losses? (Are you questioning his power? His goodness? His faithfulness? His loving-kindness?)

Father, you know the state of my heart and why it's hard for me to trust you. I ask you to help me come out of hiding and enter fully into your presence and shelter. Help me to experience your deep love and compassion for me. To know that you weep with those who weep, including me. Give me grace to rest deeply in your presence now.

Exchange your *heartache* for the shelter of Jesus's deep *compassion.*

3. God is even greater and more loving and more powerful than you have imagined. What difference would believing that make for you in your heartache?
4. Exchange your heartbreak for God's shelter by writing a prayer to the Lord, pouring out your pain, disappointment, and even anger to him. Try not to self-edit; simply pour out what you are feeling. He will sort through it all with you.

Father, I hurt so much. But the losses I have sustained are only compounded by the added loss of closeness to you. I want to return to you. Help me, please, to believe your love for me—even in the midst of my losses.

See yourself in union with Christ.

5. How might Jesus use your heartbreak to invite you to experience him in new and deeper ways?

Father, I entrust myself into your loving hands. I know I am a blood-bought and precious child of yours—you proved you are completely committed to my good when you gave me Jesus. I am yours. Give me grace right now to step into your arms and rest

deeply in your compassionate, sheltering embrace—even if I
don't see your answers this side of heaven.

Trust Christ's presence is with you.

7. Create a breath prayer that reflects your longing for fullness with
   God as your Comforter. Then turn to this prayer throughout your
   day as a reminder to trust him. (For example: "Father, I believe
   . . . help my unbelief." "Jesus, fill my heart . . . with your life."
   "Help me rest . . . in your embrace.")

PART THREE

Sharing Sacred Refuge

ARE YOU WATCHING what's happening around you? In addition to our personal crises, we are all in a time of crisis at a broader level. As the tectonic plates of our culture shift beneath our feet, we all wonder how long they will hold. We feel like we are living in a house of cards. We wonder what life will be like for future generations.

The church, in large part, has lost its voice in our culture. A spirit of fear and confusion prevails. As David cried out in his day, "If the foundations are destroyed, what can the righteous do?" (Psalm 11:3). Many today are throwing up their hands in hopelessness: "Nothing." They are longing to find—as we have—a safe place from the storms that threaten to capsize us all.

Be encouraged, sister! The testimony of Scripture is that when the days are darkening, God sends forth his light in power. One of the ways he does this is through his people. Yes, through ordinary, imperfect, messy saints like you and me. One of the key marks of God's people in the days ahead will be our peace in the midst of chaos and uncertainty. But this will only happen if we leave our false shelters and trust Jesus—and Jesus alone—to be our refuge. Not our shrinking 401(k)s. Not personal comfort. Not political clout. Not control.

In this final section of *Sacred Refuge*, we'll consider the questions, *Can God empower me to fight for others and share with them the shelter he's given me?* and *Can Jesus awaken his bride, the church, and restore our first love for him?*

It turns out there is plenty of room under the sheltering wings of the infinite and eternal One. For you. For me. For all God's children. Let's explore how, having given us a safe place in himself, God now calls us to share his sacred refuge with others. This is the final leg of our journey out of hiding in fear and into life as God's brave, beloved daughters. It is a high calling; it is hard and holy work. But as we join with Jesus in bringing God's kingdom here on earth—it just might alter the trajectory of our culture and world.

CHAPTER 9

Empowered

Finding Shelter in Our Divine Warrior

Wondrously show your steadfast love,
O Savior of those who seek refuge
from their adversaries at your right hand.
—Psalm 17:7

Can God empower me to fight for others and offer them the sacred refuge he has given me?

AFTER MY COMMUNITY had made numerous attempts over thirty years to start a pro-life work, God raised up three mothers with a shared vision of saving unborn babies' lives. As they prayed, he put the right pieces together: a young new leader to birth the work, a place to minister to women, and seed money to assist pregnant women in our community who were considering abortion.

Almost three years into the process, God brought another leader, Paige, an older woman with a personal story related to abortion, to carry on the work. A modern-day Deborah, she has arisen as "a mother in Israel" (Judges 5:7) to fight for unborn lives. Here is her story.

> If someone had told me I would be the pro-life voice in our community, I would have laughed at them. Having experienced a forced abortion at age nineteen, I could not imagine God using me to stand for life. Yet in his sovereign plan and power, that is exactly what he has done.
>
> To be honest, I was sure my abortion disqualified me from being of much use to God and others. I didn't seek a place of leadership or sign up to lead our local pregnancy resource center as executive director. But when God called me, it was unmistakable. And having called me, he also put the "yes" in me.
>
> As the leader of a local pregnancy center, I stand for truth in a world full of lies. Not just truth about abortion, but the

truth of the gospel. Our pregnancy center is founded on the truth that in love Jesus Christ came to earth to bridge the gulf between a holy God and us, his rebellious children. We believe the only way to truly save a life—whether it is the life of an unborn child or the life of a mother—is to point them to Christ. The same gospel that sheltered me in God's forgiveness after my abortion speaks life to the women we now seek to shelter.

God has provided everything needed for this battle. He has given us the step-by-step strategy we have needed to fight for life in our county. His plan is always better than ours, and we listen carefully for him to speak and lead—and then we follow.

He has gathered once-isolated individuals into a unified force of forty-four churches gathered for life and for the gospel. I think it is safe to say that our work is bringing about human flourishing in our county. Community life is richer, deeper, and more joyful because of our life-giving work:

More than seven hundred women have chosen life instead of death. More than four hundred fifty women have received resources and equipment for their motherhood journey. At least eight women have come into a saving relationship with Jesus Christ, the true Life-giver. He has given them what they need to shelter and nurture the life inside them.

Many look at me and say, "Good job, Paige. You lead well." I know the truth. It is God who leads, God who speaks, God who gathers, God who saves, and God who gives power for the victories we see. This is his work, accomplished in his power, for his glory.

Fighting Our Sense of Inadequacy

Like Paige, we may be all too aware of our own weakness. We often feel disqualified from taking action and tempted to skulk away from the battle. Many have.

But as those who have discovered how to abide in God's sacred refuge, our response can be different. As restored life-givers, we can shift our focus onto God's mighty power as our Divine Warrior and begin to fight the growing darkness of our day. We can dare to ask, as our sister Paige did, "What might God do *through me*?"

I don't know the past you struggle with, or the present limitations you see when you look in the mirror. You may feel completely inadequate and wonder if you really have anything to offer. But God doesn't feel that way when he looks at you. He sees a woman whose broken and uneven journey—when given to him—offers something unique and important to our world at this moment.

The world is waiting for you—for all of us in the church—to come out of hiding in fear. It is time for us to step out of the shadows and into the good works God has prepared in advance for us to walk in (Ephesians 2:10).

Where do we begin? We've spent much time reflecting on how we can seek refuge in Jesus's loving presence. What if, having been sheltered there, we learned how to live and minister from that place—where God dwells in the midst of our brokenness? Many of us have barely begun to acknowledge the question burning in our hearts: "Can God empower me to arise against the effects of evil in my day and shelter others?" Be encouraged by God's answer to this question in the life of one of our sacred sisters.

Deborah's Story

In the book of Judges we meet Deborah, an ancient sister whom God used to win a decisive battle against evil and restore peace to her people for an entire generation.

To say that it was unusual for a woman in ancient Israel to rise to a place of leadership is an understatement. But Deborah's gender did not disqualify her from God using her at a critical moment in Israel's history. In fact, she was just the woman for the job.

Deborah's story unfolds in Palestine, about 1100 BC. A hundred or so years earlier, Joshua had led the nation of Israel into the land of Canaan, directed by God to destroy the pagan nations that inhabited the land promised to his people. Although Israel displaced many of those tribes, they left some of them unconquered.

The result? Generations later, those same Canaanite tribes and their kings caused disaster in the lives of the Israelites. Worse than that, the tribes' pagan practices and idolatry infected God's holy people. In short, Israel became "Canaanized." The writer of Judges described the long-term effect of idolatry this way: "Everyone did what was right in his own eyes" (Judges 21:25). Calling out the issue in no uncertain terms, Deborah named the root of the problem: "When new gods were chosen, then war was in the gates" (5:8).

Deborah came onto the scene when Israel was in full-blown apostasy. There was no priesthood carrying out the sacrifices to cover the nation's sin. There was no king, and the people had abandoned Jehovah as their ruler. Israel's army was ragtag at best.

In short, the nation was in crisis. Having sheltered Deborah in his Word and filled her with his wisdom, God appointed her to lead his people into a sacred refuge that he would build for them.

Her story is told in Judges 4, and her song in Judges 5 recounts the mighty acts of God.

If Deborah could sit beside us and tell her story, it might sound something like this:

For years I had read and memorized the book of the law, the Word God breathed through Moses for his people to live by. I savored its truths and loved its ability to cut a straight path through complex situations and troubling arguments.

People had been coming to me for years to settle disputes;

they trusted my impartiality. So when God called me to act as Israel's judge, I was well prepared. I sat atop a hill under what became known as "Deborah's Palm." From that vantage point, ruling at the geographical center of the nation, I was an eyewitness to the oppressive, devastating effects of idolatry among my people. When the people abandoned Jehovah and chose new gods, war came to our gates.

By following the gods of the land, Israel had put themselves under the thumb of Canaanite king Jabin. His five-star general was a mercenary enforcer named Sisera. Together they had amassed an overwhelming physical force of nine hundred iron chariots.

I watched for twenty years as Sisera and his horde rolled into Israel's towns, taking what they wanted and mowing down anything—or anyone—in their path. Terrified villagers stayed away from the main roads for fear of being killed. Attacked one time too many, farmers abandoned their once-fertile fields, and people went hungry.

Trade ground to a halt. There was no busy marketplace or public square where people traded goods and ideas. The economy was in shambles. Crime was rampant, so people took roundabout paths. The sound of music and wedding celebrations? Gone.

Times were dark and getting darker every day. The richness of community life was banished, replaced by fear and utter isolation. And all the result of God's people choosing other gods.

I knew all this hurt God's heart, and it bruised mine. A holy indignation began to rise in me. My husband, Lappidoth, and I had many discussions about the deterioration of our nation and prayed fervently for Jehovah to come to our aid.

Finally, when the people could take no more, they cried out and asked Jehovah to rescue them.

One day, I sensed God's presence more deeply than ever

before. Matters were coming to a head. He wanted me to call Barak, Israel's military leader, into action against Sisera. Jehovah also called me to accompany him into battle.

"But, Lord," I replied, "I am only a woman."

But it was my very design as a woman God most wanted to use in this season of Israel's distress. My innate capacity for life-giving. My emotional discernment. My ability to gather and bring consensus among people and families. These would now be needed to galvanize whole tribes—indeed an entire nation—toward defeating Sisera. It was time to free our people from his oppression once and for all!

Who would have guessed that what I thought disqualified me from God's service was the very thing he rejoiced to use?

So I summoned Barak the son of Abinoam from Kedesh-naphtali. I said to him, "Hasn't the God of Israel already commanded you to go and gather your men at Mount Tabor, taking ten thousand from the people of Naphtali and the people of Zebulun?"

> ## Who would have guessed that what I thought disqualified me from God's service was the very thing he rejoiced to use?

God gave the strategy: "And I will draw out Sisera, the general of Jabin's army, to meet you by the river Kishon with his chariots and his troops." Then God made this astounding promise: "And I will give him into your hand."

God had already called Barak, a military leader in Israel, to engage Sisera in battle. But Barak hadn't deployed the troops, which, after twenty years of oppression, economic hardship, and intimidation, were not battle ready. The tribes were

scattered and cowering, some with little more than farming
implements for weapons.

But they were not the only reluctant warriors. Barak himself told me, "If you will go with me, Deborah, I will go. But if
you don't go with me, I'm not going." I agreed, but told Barak
that although God would go into battle on Israel's behalf,
Barak's hesitancy would cost him the bragging rights for this
victory. They would go instead to a woman (Jael, most blessed
of women).

Barak and I then had to muster the scattered tribes of Israel to lead them into what most of them perceived to be a
suicide mission. Many did not answer the call, but some of the
tribes, including Issachar, Benjamin, Zebulun, and Ephraim
(my tribe) and Naphtali (Barak's tribe), did respond. What a
glorious sight it was to see them streaming toward Mt. Tabor!

Word reached Sisera that ten thousand Israelites were on
the move and heading to Mt. Tabor for a big showdown. As
he called on his charioteers and fighting men to head to that
location, I spoke the encouraging word from God that Barak
most needed to hear at that moment: "Rise up! For this is the
day the LORD has given Sisera into your power. Hasn't the
LORD already gone out before you?"

From the top of Mt. Tabor, located in the northeast part
of the Jezreel Valley, Barak led his men down into the Kishon
River Valley—straight into Sisera and his massive iron chariots. That was when we saw the power of Jehovah!

God sent confusion among Sisera's troops. He also sent
a thunderstorm and torrential rain, all of which ran down
the slopes of Mt. Tabor. As Israel's army advanced down the
mountain toward Sisera's massive forces, they were sure they
were running toward their own bloodbath.

But what use are nine hundred iron chariots when rain
turns dry land into rivers of sludge?

In a dramatic turn of events, Sisera's weapons of mass destruction were—literally—stuck in the mud. His men became sitting ducks, unable to escape the ten thousand armed men led by Barak and me, who led Issachar. Barak's army may have been outnumbered by Sisera's nine hundred chariots, but make no mistake: Sisera didn't stand a chance against our mighty God!

The Lord routed Sisera and all his chariots and army before Barak by the edge of the sword. Completely undone, the mighty Sisera ran away from the battlefield. Unknowingly, he headed straight to his doom at the hands of a crafty woman named Jael.

Who would have thought it? God used Jael and me—two women—as part of his plan to bring Sisera down. And yet, for anyone who'd ever been empowered by God's strength, it came as no surprise that he can use anyone he pleases to accomplish his work.

Arising as Mothers

Sister, isn't it encouraging to read an account of such remarkable female leadership—even though women were often disregarded in ancient cultures? Let's be clear, though: Deborah's story isn't a call for female empowerment for its own sake. As those who live by God's strength, let's not settle for the world's definition of power. It's far too weak.

Chairing the building committee at church. Managing a multi-tiered corporate team. Leading change as an online influencer. These are all great callings, but they won't bring about lasting change until they are empowered by our unique capacity as women to bring forth God's life in the world. Carrying, birthing, nurturing, protecting, and fighting for life (whether physical or spiritual) are women's superpowers because they are integral to our God-given design. When women rise up as God's life-givers in these callings, we will see his kingdom advance mightily!

> ## As those who live by God's strength, let's not settle for the world's definition of power. It's far too weak.

It's evident Deborah herself understood this. As she recounted the work God did through her and Barak to save the nation, Deborah made no mention of her impressive credentials. She could have listed any or all of them: wise judge, God's mouthpiece, prophetess, military advisor, or even warrior. She didn't. The one word Deborah used to describe her role of supreme usefulness to God and her people was "mother" (Judges 5:7).

Notice, too, that she didn't say, "I was *only* a mother." She proudly proclaims: "I arose a mother."

Interestingly, the Hebrew word for *mother* means "glue of the family." Any of us who keep track of a busy family's schedule, plan the birthday parties and holiday gatherings, connect our family's generations, or comfort hurting children know that "holding things together" is a pretty good description for mothering.

But Deborah wasn't talking about physical nurturing. She was talking about spiritual mothering, fostering relational connection—to God and then others. In her book *Spiritual Mothering*, Susan Hunt defines spiritual mothering as happening "when a woman possessing faith and spiritual maturity enters into a nurturing relationship with a younger woman in order to encourage and equip her to live for God's glory."[1] In her book's practical treatment of Titus 2:3–5, Hunt lays the scriptural foundation for mothering beyond the birthing of physical children.

What if, taking Deborah's cue, we pan out to a broader application of spiritual mothering? I believe the needs of our day call for spiritual mothering that starts in our primary relationships (spouses, children, grandchildren, parents) and then extends to others (neighbors, people at work, younger women, youth and seniors in our communities, and beyond). It won't look the same for all of us, but based on the gifts and opportunities God gives us, we can arise as spiritual mothers in our day. Sister, we can *find* refuge in God and then learn to *abide* there. But until we *share* sacred refuge with others, we won't fulfill God's calling for us as spiritual life-givers.

Sheltered by Jesus, Our Divine Warrior

It may be hard for us to picture Deborah amid the battle. Or even in a position of leadership that prompted Barak and the whole nation into battle. Was she afraid, we wonder? She must have been. Nonetheless, Deborah's obedience to God's call teaches us much.

Saying yes to God does not mean we suddenly become super-human. Deep dependence on him as our power source emboldens us. Then God's courage motivates the action we take, even if our knees are shaking. We step out in obedience, regardless of how we feel, trusting that he who called us is faithful. We trust that our Divine Warrior can empower us to fight the battles before us and find victory.

Many of the biblical women we've met so far hid in one false shelter or another. But that wasn't the case with Deborah. So what was it Deborah had learned about God that empowered her to face this life-and-death conflict? What does her example teach us as modern women navigating a world plagued by our own version of terrorism and cultural disintegration?

The Secret to Victory

Deborah was able to stand strong and face her battles for three reasons.

First, she knew her God. She had walked with him for years, road testing his promises, seeking his wise counsel, and finding him faithful.

She was steeped in the law Jehovah gave to Moses, leading wisely from God's Word. Deborah had learned to discern the voice of God.

Second, Deborah knew God could use anyone to fulfill his purposes. So when he instructed her to call Barak to battle, she didn't demur and say, "Who, little old me? Surely you don't want a woman to lead this fight?" and duck quietly out the back door. No, when God called her name, she obeyed wholeheartedly, knowing that her Divine Warrior would shelter her in the coming conflict.

Finally, Deborah knew how high the stakes were in the battle God called her to join. Deborah left the sheltering palm tree from where she judged Israel and joined the battle because her heart became broken for what broke (and angered) God's heart: the destruction of his people. Deborah couldn't stand by and watch her people and her nation being decimated any longer. Israel was in a disastrous state *until* Deborah arose as a mother for her people to push back evil. God empowered her to arise a mother not of a single family, but an entire nation!

Had Deborah not been faithful to God's call, village life would have continued to deteriorate. But because of Deborah's faithful obedience, Judges 5:31 tells us that "the land had rest for forty years." For a people who had been mired in skirmishes and hardship for years, this was a sweet victory indeed.

Sheltered, to Shelter Others

God empowered Deborah to become a life-giver and a life-nurturer. In Judges 5:7, Deborah said that village life had ceased until she "arose" a mother in Israel. She lamented the loss of close family circles, community life, celebrations, and connection among people, which were all being replaced with isolation and fear. The word *arose* in the Hebrew is *qûm*. It appears over 628 times in 596 Old Testament verses and can be translated in a variety of ways, including "stand," "establish," "help," "fulfill," "strengthen," "lift up," and "accomplish."[2]

When we arise, we come out of self-dependence and ask God to guide and empower us. Here's what this can look like in our day:

- Waking up and moving out of complacency.
- Standing up and saying, "No more."
- Establishing truth in the public square.
- Making good what has started to decay.
- Holding those who hurt.
- Enduring hardship and persecution.
- Persisting in doing good.
- Performing unglamorous tasks with faithfulness.
- Lifting up the refugee and the homeless.
- Rousing the half-hearted.
- Accomplishing the impossible with the strength God supplies.

As in Deborah's day, our culture is running after other gods. The evidence is irrefutable; the consequences are inescapable. The battles we are engaged in at this moment for our culture and the world are the result of idolatry, exacerbated by God's people hunkering down in isolation and fear. Village life is deteriorating. Our economy teeters on the edge of ruin. The church has, in large part, forgotten its call to be salt and light in our culture.

Arising as God's Beloved Warriors
The need is great. The time is now.

Picture our culture as a vast fabric of relationships and alliances. At our best, we experience security in the perpendicular strength of warp against weft in our inter-woven connections. But with every divorce, trafficked child, abortion, church split, school shooting, or business failure, we hear the sound of the individual threads that hold us together snapping. How long until the whole thing is nothing but shreds?

Today we watch in fear as those connections are broken and conflict among us escalates. As Deborah explained, "When new gods were chosen, then war was in the gates" (Judges 5:8). What have our culture's idols of personal pleasure and comfort, power, and affluence cost our communities? Nothing less than family unity, faithful friendships, genuine presence, kindness, honesty, justice, hope, and equality, to name a few.

But God is at work, sister! God has made us life-givers. That means our inner radars hit high alert when we see the disintegration of our country, culture, and world. And let's be clear: the real enemy isn't people—including those who live or see things differently than we do—it's Satan. As Paul pointed out in Ephesians 6:12: "For we do not wrestle against flesh and blood, but against the rulers, against the authorities, against the cosmic powers over this present darkness, against the spiritual forces of evil in the heavenly places." The enemy loves it when we cut down other image-bearers of God. But our battle is not *against* them, but *for* them against the evil principalities and powers that are stealing their lives. We fight, as Jesus did, by loving people back to life.

When God shows us the effects of sin (death, disintegration, destruction) in and around us, our calling is to ask him, "Lord, how would you have me bring your life into this situation?"

We fight, as Jesus did, by loving people back to life.

Paige arises as the leader of her local crisis pregnancy center. Luanne cares for her grandchildren so her daughter can work as a physician. Krista starts an after-school tutoring program at her church. Ari mentors refugee women from an underserved part of her community. Daneisha offers sewing classes to women in her neighborhood and shares Jesus with them as part of the lessons. Carly runs for a seat on her local school board. Evie pursues a degree in counseling so she can serve hurting marriages and families in her community. Deirdre initiates a public arts program to beautify public spaces. Jen leads a Bible study at her office. Maria teaches middle schoolers how to grow food in a community garden. Jennifer runs a soup kitchen to feed the hungry in her community.

In short, each woman shares sacred refuge by sheltering others with the love and intentionality of the One who has sheltered her.

This is not about doing a huge thing for God. It's about starting small and reweaving the part of the fabric that has torn right where we live. (Think of Nehemiah and his people rebuilding their small part of the broken wall of Jerusalem.) God doesn't despise the day of small beginnings (Zechariah 4:10) and neither should we. He's not looking for the impressive, just those who are available and obedient. God will do all the heavy lifting—supplying the resources, strategy, and helpers to obey his call, just as he did in Deborah's day.

> **TRANSFORMING TRUTH**
>
> Inadequacy taunts us with, "Who do you think you are? What possible difference can you make?" We must turn away from its lies and tune in to the voice who calls out, "Beloved, I am in you and with you, empowering you to arise as my anointed life-giver in a dying world."

Sister, this is what I wonder: What might God do through his daughters as we listen to and obey his Word—arising as powerful life-givers to children, families, neighborhoods, schools, churches, communities, companies, and cultures?

I believe this can be our finest hour. Consider what eighteenth-century historian and poet Matthew Arnold wrote: "If ever the world sees a time when women shall come together purely and simply for the benefit and good of mankind, it will be a power such as the world has never seen."[3]

How much more might be accomplished for God's glory as his daughters follow the lead of Jesus Christ, our victorious Divine Warrior? What if we followed him into a battle fought with the weapons of sacrificial love and self-denying service for others? What lives might be saved—and redirected—for the kingdom? What healing and restoration might God work among us?

Having soundly beaten our enemy, Christ has made us more than conquerors in himself (Romans 8:37). Just as God told Deborah about the final victory he would bring over Sisera, we know the final outcome of the battle against evil. And from this place of victorious hope, as daughters of Deborah, we are empowered to arise in our own day.

Enter the Sacred Refuge of God's Mighty Power

Jesus may be saying something like this to you:

> Beloved, I know your heart. I see the fear that has crept unnoticed into your mind. It steals your peace and causes you to hole up in your own small world as a safe place to ride out the current cultural storm. But I tell you now, it is time to leave behind your fears and insecurities.
>
> It is time to come out of hiding where it's more comfortable and less risky.
>
> All you see is your inadequacy, but I have designed you as a life-giver. This is your original purpose—now fully redeemed and empowered by me. I have created you to shelter and protect others. Your deepest desire, though you hardly dare admit it, is to arise as a life-giving change-maker in these darkening days.
>
> Begin by praying. Ask for wisdom and my strategy for your part in this battle. Find the others in your family, your church, and your community who are also done with sitting passively while the enemy continues to steal, kill, and destroy.
>
> Band with them in a united front against lies that are causing the slow and steady decay of your "village life" and the captivity they are bringing to your children and grandchildren.
>
> You will need power for this season of spiritual attack in order to not only fight but prevail in this battle. Know this, beloved: In your own strength, you are unequal to the warfare ahead. Only I have the power to bring you through to victory.

The battle is mine, not yours. So it is essential that you keep your eyes locked on me and fight with the strategy I give. Walk forward, listening and obeying, listening and obeying, and in this way you will go from strength to strength.

I know your knees are knocking. I see your hand shaking as you take up the sword of the Spirit, daughter. You are fighting the voice that attacks you even now: "Who do you think you are? Are you really ready to take on this fight? Go back to your distracted and drowsy existence before things get ugly."

Here is your response to the lies that voice speaks. Remember exactly who you are in me. Rehearse it: "I am a blood-bought child of the King of Kings. As his beloved daughter, I now put on the whole armor of God. United to Christ, I am more than a conqueror. His banner over me is love, and as part of Christ's church, I enter the enemy's territory with Christ's love as my greatest weapon. I trust his promise that even the gates of hell will not prevail against us!"

Beloved, live in the truths of these words. Plant them in your mind and establish them deeply inside your spirit each day. Only then will you be able to follow me into battle when I call you to "arise, daughter of Deborah!"[4]

REST Under His Wings
Spend time quieting yourself in God's presence.

Release control.
1. What problems in your world, nation, or community cause you concern? Are there ways you hide from God by turning to other people/things/strategies to help you cope with these concerns?
2. What might it look like to take your worry about these issues to God?

*Father, you know what keeps me up at night, the mounting prob-
lems all around us. Carrying it all is going to undo me. Instead, I
put all my concerns and anxieties into your capable hands. Will
you please carry it all and give me peace that you are still on
your throne and at work in ways I don't yet see?*

Exchange your *weakness* for Christ's mighty *power.*
3. What life circumstances or doubts make you feel unequipped to
   do anything about the problems you see around you?
4. How might God be calling you to "arise as a mother" for a person
   (or people) in your community? What unique gifts, interests, or
   dreams has he placed in you?

*Lord, you know how I struggle with a deep sense of inadequacy.
But your Word is full of examples of weak people you chose to
use in powerful ways. Right now, I lay down my fears of failure
and exchange my weakness for your might. Please empower me
to arise as a life-giver in the midst of my ailing culture!*

See yourself in union with Christ.
5. How does knowing you carry Christ's presence with you make a
   difference for how you go into battle to help set others free?

*Father, I ask you to show me the first step you would have me
take to share sacred refuge with others. Show me the specific
way you would have me live from refuge as your brave, beloved
daughter. Help me to serve others sacrificially with the strength
you provide!*

Trust Christ as the one who empowers you to arise.
6. Create a breath prayer that reflects your longing for change with
   God as your Divine Warrior and power source. Then turn to this
   prayer throughout your day as a reminder to trust in him. (For

example: "Sheltered in your love . . . help me to shelter others."
"Help me to see . . . where you call me to arise." "Give me faith . . .
to fight the battle.")

(To discover how to band with other women to fulfill God's
call together, go to appendix A, "What Is Sacred Sisterhood?"
on p. 229.)

CHAPTER 10

Beloved

Finding Shelter in the Arms of the Bridegroom

Keep me as the apple of your eye;
hide me in the shadow of your wings.
—Psalm 17:8

Can Jesus awaken his bride, the church, and restore our first love for him?

THESE DAYS, IF you drive north into a certain small Midwestern town, you'll find something missing—the strip joint that occupied seventeen acres in the prime "Welcome to our town" spot for almost thirty years. The building was hidden behind trees, but glaring signs boldly announced where, in the name of entertainment, sin could be celebrated, lives broken, relationships shattered, and souls corrupted.

It made many avert or shield their eyes when driving into or out of town. It also made a friend of mine pray, "Lord, all it would take is a single lightning bolt and you could burn that place down. Please?" Her heart ached for the women who thought they had no other option to earn money to feed their kids and pay their rent. She knew some customers intentionally chose debauchery. Others were lured to it, almost against their will.

So my friend prayed for the lightning bolt (or other means of massive fire) for decades.

But God didn't answer her prayer. At least, not the way she expected.

Instead, he sent a handful of women from her church to provide a breath of kindness, acts of generosity, and gifts of beauty to the dancers in the club. Once a week for a couple of years, they took cookies or muffins to the dancers, offered to paint their nails or do their hair, volunteered to provide childcare or after-school care for their kids, and even asked the owner if they could brighten up the dancers' dressing room.

The skeptical owner tolerated the team's presence after he realized they truly did have no other motive than serving and loving. But he wasn't about to pay for paint and new curtains for the girls who worked for him. The team from church insisted they only needed his permission. They'd provide all the equipment, paint, and labor.

"Why would you do that?"

"We care."

Years of weekly visits and kindness with no agenda (other than the women's unspoken sense that theirs was a love assignment from God). Years of listening rather than preaching. Years of providing the dancers an hour or two of being noticed and cared for, of unexpected friendship.

Still, it shocked everyone when the owner one day called the pastor and said, "I want your church to buy my property. This isn't the legacy I want to leave for my children."

A church purchasing a strip joint? How does a pastor approach the elder board with that request? However, the congregation, even without the financial means, unanimously agreed that God had to be behind the request. He is, after all, the Redeemer. They said yes and raised enough money in one push to make the down payment.

The now-previous owner was driving the bulldozer the day the building was razed, all evidence of its former purposes removed, scraped clean. Even the dirt on which it had stood was redeemed, covered in grass seed and prayer.

Already, the community was finding solutions for the questions asked: "The women are out of work. How can we provide scholarships for trade school or college? How can we business people find them employment they can be proud of? What do they need?"

Today, when travelers pass that spot on the way into town, they see a lush, green oasis that serves as a community gathering place, an open-air worship venue, a concert location.

I wonder what the former dancers feel when they drive past that memory. No doubt their answer includes the word *freedom*. And it began with Jesus's unconditional love expressed through the local church.

A Runaway Bride: Church in Crisis

This example of Spirit-birthed love and service is rare. Sadly, it's not what's being experienced in many American churches. In fact, a disturbing trend is playing out instead: many are leaving the church—not growing it through selfless service. "We are currently experiencing the largest and fastest religious shift in US history. It is greater than the First and Second Great Awakening and every revival in our country combined but in the opposite direction," reports Missio Nexus.[1]

I have been a pastor's wife for decades. In addition to that, my work takes me every month to a new destination in the Southeast US, where my goal is to build relationships with churches in my region whom God has motivated to partner with the ministry I serve. I have had a front-row seat from which to view this shift.

I have heard the heartache of pastors and global outreach directors as they experienced hard transitions in their churches and ministries during the pandemic and its aftermath. In March 2020, I remember thinking, "The church has left the building."

Sadly, some never returned. Barna Research discovered that in recent years, 32 percent of former church attendees simply stopped going to church (in person or virtually) altogether.[2]

We may be dealing with personal crises of various kinds. But our sister, the church, is in a crisis all her own.

What is most concerning is that many who have left the church used to be insiders. "These aren't the 'nones' who have no religious affiliation. They're the 'dones' who've been faithfully serving in local churches for years."[3] Their exit is only one symptom of the deeper issues we face as the body of Christ, caused less by external circumstances than the state of our hearts before God.

Many of us in the church have lost our first love for Jesus. As such, we resemble the character Maggie Carpenter (played by Julia Roberts) in the rom-com *Runaway Bride*. She flees one fiancé after another at the altar because, it turns out, she doesn't know who she is.

> ## We may be dealing with personal crises of various kinds. But our sister, the church, is in a crisis all her own.

Without a clear sense of our identities in Christ, how have we become a runaway bride? Are we falling for the fallacy that success in the local church equals impressive numbers and flashy public ministry? Have we pursued cultural relevancy to the point of losing the message of the gospel? And in times such as these rife with conflict over who will hold power, have we pursued worldly influence instead of the kind of power Jesus wielded through death to self and sacrificial love for others? I wonder, sister, is this something you notice in your own faith community? Is its root cause our own identity crisis as members of Christ's body?

The good news is that as the church, we have a Bridegroom who tells us exactly who we are. He sees our faithfulness, as well as our spiritual adulteries, and still calls us his beloved. This gives us hope that the current state of the church is not our final state.

In fact, I believe God is offering us a whole new way of being the church.

Instead of being a runaway bride, we are called by God to become a bride who knows and loves her Bridegroom intimately and longs for his return. As we respond to God's wooing during this season of shaking, may our hearts fall out of love with political clout, success as proof of worth, personal peace and comfort, and the other lovers that have captured our attentions.

In the light of our Bridegroom's passionate affection for us, all other loves will lose their alluring power. May the current phenomenon of "dechurching" become instead a fresh movement of "rechurching." May we stop hiding from our Bridegroom and instead lean into the sacred refuge he offers.

Amid our dechurching crisis, encouraging examples of healthy churches are emerging. As the previous story reminds us, beautiful things happen when women minister from their identities as the beloved of Jesus. Having been sheltered by him, our Midwestern sisters offered sacred refuge to others. What might happen in *your* community if the bride of Christ were to return to her first love?

The Bride of Christ: Our "Sister" in Sacred Refuge

Has anyone ever written a love poem for you? This is exactly what we have in the Song of Solomon. This poetic book inspired by the Holy Spirit expresses passion and sexual desire in a couple's marriage relationship. Bible scholars agree, however, that it also points to the mutual longing for intimacy between the bride (the church) and her Bridegroom, Jesus Christ.

Let's listen to the voice of the beloved (the bride) in the second chapter of Song of Solomon 2:8–9:

> The voice of my beloved!
>   Behold, he comes,
> leaping over the mountains,
>   bounding over the hills.
> My beloved is like a gazelle
>   or a young stag.
> Behold, there he stands
>   behind our wall,

> gazing through the windows,
>   looking through the lattice.

Can you hear the excitement in verses 8 and 9? This is a bride who knows the sound of her lover's voice (John 10:27). She is tuned to its timbre and can read its tone. The lover calls her name, and her heart jumps at the sound.

Sadly, this isn't always how we respond to our Lover, Jesus. When we hide from him, Jesus's love for us is unrequited. If we as the bride of Christ will respond to his invitation to intimacy, I believe our days of crisis will be over.

In this passage, the beloved not only hears but also sees her lover. Using the simile "like a gazelle or a young stag," the bride tells us all we need to know about the one she loves: he is agile, fleet of foot, athletic, and heading her way! Nothing will impede his progress toward her—not even mountains or hills. Having made his way to her, he stands outside her home and gazes through the lattice, not as a stalker, but as a seeker of her presence. He longs so deeply for her that he must draw near to her.

But there are barriers between them, obstacles to their union, that the Bridegroom must overcome. In his commentary on the Song of Solomon, Iain Duguid says, "There is a heavenly Bridegroom who doesn't just gaze at us longingly from a distance, but bursts through the walls that we have erected to keep him out so that he can sweep us off our feet."

Why is the Bridegroom so powerfully motivated? He is in love and seeking union with his beloved bride. Duguid continues, "The powerful sexual drives God has given us to cement us together in marriage are but a pale reflection of just how passionately and intensely God desires to be bonded to us."[4] Beloved of God, Jesus is pursuing us!

The Lover Who Calls You out of Hiding

We have heard from the bride. Now we hear the Bridegroom speak in Song of Solomon 2:10–13:

Arise, my love, my beautiful one,
> and come away,
for behold, the winter is past;
> the rain is over and gone.
The flowers appear on the earth,
> the time of singing has come,
and the voice of the turtledove
> is heard in our land.
The fig tree ripens its figs,
> and the vines are in blossom;
> they give forth fragrance.
Arise, my love, my beautiful one,
> and come away.

In verse 10, the same lover who has pursued his bride past every obstacle begins to speak, his words reflecting the deep longing of his heart. He calls the object of his affection "*my* love" and "*my* beautiful one." As Christ's bride, we belong exclusively to him. We are blood-bought. But how can he call us (who still struggle with sin) "beautiful"? It is because the Bridegroom has clothed us in his glorious righteousness (Isaiah 61:10).

Sister, can you hear the longing in the Bridegroom's heart for us, his beautiful ones, to draw near? His love for us, even now, can empower us to arise, which is the clear command and central invitation of his song. The word *arise* carries with it a variety of possible meanings, some of which have powerful implications as the call and command of the Bridegroom to his church: "rise up," "abide," "make good," "hold," "endure," "rouse up," "strengthen," and "succeed."[5]

Awakening to the Bridegroom's Call

In a season when the church has been significantly distracted from the Bridegroom, the words from Song of Solomon take on deep significance. Even now, we can hear the Bridegroom's voice calling to us in our crisis of cultural marginalization and lukewarm devotion. If we obey his call to arise and reawaken to his love, he will catalyze powerful, Spirit-birthed change through his bride:

- *Abide* deeply in me, for apart from me you can do nothing (John 15:4–5).
- *Establish* yourselves as my holy people (Deuteronomy 28:9).
- *Stand*, having put on the full armor of God (Ephesians 6:13–17).
- *Accomplish* the good works I have prepared in advance for you (Ephesians 2:10).
- *Rise up* and build (Nehemiah 2:18).
- As salt and light, *make good* again that which has become corrupt (Matthew 5:13–16).
- *Help* the least of these (Matthew 25:40–45).
- *Endure* hardship and persecution for my sake (2 Timothy 2:3).

> **TRANSFORMING TRUTH**
>
> When the voices of other lovers seek to entice you, listen for the voice of your Bridegroom, who invites you into deeper intimacy: "Come to me, my beautiful beloved. Enter into this new season by receiving my tender embrace—now and forever."

But none of this will happen unless we first hear and heed the Bridegroom's initial call in Song of Solomon 2:10 to "come away" with him. There are so many things vying for our time and attention in today's world—so many ways to look for identity and worth outside of our first love. But the Bridegroom beckons us to return to him.

At a personal level, this is Jesus's call to each of us to come spend time with him. As Christ's bride, let us be wholly his. In a broader sense, this is Jesus's call for the church to part company with whatever has distracted us from his presence and power. He's calling us to nothing less than seeking him, collectively, with our whole heart, soul, mind, and strength (Mark 12:30).

A New Season Dawns

In Song of Solomon 2:11–13, the Bridegroom expands on the invitation for his beloved to "come away" with him. He invites us to "behold" with him a significant change of season: "The winter is past; the rain is over and gone." He is pointing out an important shift. The Bridegroom is saying, in a sense, "The winter was hard. Cold and rain kept us from each other. But now spring has come, and with it, a new opportunity for us to be together." Using rich imagery that engages our senses (the appearance of flowers, the sound of singing and the cooing of the turtledove, the taste of figs, and the sweet aroma of blossoming vines), the Bridegroom draws us closer still.

Having called us to arise and come to him, in verse 14, the Bridegroom continues to woo us with a deeper insight into the state of his heart: he misses us.

> O my dove, in the clefts of the rock,
>   in the crannies of the cliff,
> let me see your face,
>   let me hear your voice,
> for your voice is sweet,
>   and your face is lovely.

The Bridegroom calls us out of the "clefts" and "crannies" where we hide from him. He wants us to shelter in him so we may enjoy a deeper closeness than ever before.

Sister, what do the "clefts" and "crannies" look like in your life? What are your hiding places? If you're like me, perhaps it's media. I can get lost in books or movies. I'm easily distracted by my phone. Facebook, Instagram, Pinterest, reels, podcasts—it's all there waiting to capture my attention. Forty minutes later, I come up for air and realize I haven't consciously spent ten minutes in God's presence all day.

Perhaps we pour all our energy into human relationships: marriage, kids, parents, in-laws. These are all precious gifts, but none of them can meet our deepest needs for connection and love. Or what about hiding in busyness? Been there; done that. Work, travel, school, projects, church, gatherings, celebrations. It's all good, but have we gotten so caught up in the whirlwind that we haven't invited the Lover of our souls into the middle of it all?

The Bridegroom calls us out of the "clefts" and "crannies" where we hide from him.

When the dust settles and we realize we've abandoned our first love for so many lesser loves, are we just too embarrassed to come back to him in confession? Have we believed the enemy's lie that Jesus is so disappointed with us that we are better off going through the motions in our relationships with him—but from a safe distance?

Or maybe we have an issue with his lordship. We hide because we prefer our own desires to his. Full surrender to him will cost us everything. Though bought at a price (1 Corinthians 6:20), we still tenaciously grasp the deed to our own lives.

Here's where I have struggled: Jesus is a wild Lover. A passion as fierce as his threatens to undo me—so I sometimes hide from intimacy from him. Perhaps you can relate.

Sister, it's time for us to stop dating Jesus. Stop allowing distractions to draw us away from him. Stop hedging our bets. With such a Lover as Jesus, who has given himself wholly to us, can we offer him any less?

Whatever the cause of our hiding, can we hear the Bridegroom's voice calling to us in the "clefts" and "crannies" we have run to? Even now he says, "Let me see your face," for "your face is lovely." He sings to us, "Let me hear your voice," for "your voice is sweet." Can you hear it? You are being wooed.

Are you tired, as I am, of all the hiding and distractions? Does your heart yearn for a new season with Jesus in which more of his life bursts forth? Jesus is stirring us. He is reawakening a fresh love in our spirits, like the first tiny buds bursting from fertile ground as the warm winds of spring begin to blow. How will we respond?

Catching the Little Foxes

As we continue to read Song of Solomon, the Bridegroom reveals the setting for our relationship in verse 15. We are in a vineyard:

> Catch the foxes for us,
>   the little foxes
> that spoil the vineyards,
>   for our vineyards are in blossom.

The image of a vineyard is prevalent elsewhere in Scripture. It is used to illustrate abiding in Christ, fruitfulness, grace, the gardener's pruning, and even disobedience (John 15:1–5). Here, however, the image warns of a threat to the vineyard's harvest. "Little foxes" are afoot, seeking to do mischief.

Old Testament scholar Tremper Longman quotes F. Landy in his commentary on the Song of Solomon: "Foxes are guileful, riddling creatures in fable and proverb; and thus comparable to the cunning serpent. . . . The presence of the foxes implies a threat to the relationship."[6]

In this fertile season of spring, at the very moment when blossoms promising life and joy are blooming throughout the vineyard, a grave threat has arisen. What's at stake here is nothing less than the survival—and fruitfulness—of the relationship between Bridegroom and bride. Left unchecked, the foxes will eat the tender blossoms and spoil the vineyard. And if they do, there will be no harvest, no wine, no wedding celebration.

The sad truth is many "little foxes" threaten our relationship with the Bridegroom. Many distractions have stolen our attention from Jesus as our first love. As our hearts are captured by the "little foxes," there is less room for the One who first loved us, and our passionate affection for Jesus cools. In time, thinking that we are rich and that we have prospered and need nothing, we become lukewarm (Revelation 3:16–17).

LITTLE FOXES IN THE CHURCH

What exactly *are* these "little foxes" that are stealing our fruitfulness as the church of Jesus Christ? They are nothing less than the idols that have captured our hearts. A study from Lifeway Research indicates that more than half of US Protestant pastors say the following "idols . . . have significant influence on their congregations":

- Comfort (67 percent)
- Control/Security (56 percent)
- Money (55 percent)
- Approval (51 percent)
- Success (49 percent)
- Social Influence (46 percent)
- Political Power (39 percent)
- Sex/Romantic Love (32 percent)[7]

It's tempting to think of current cultural trends as a huge, insurmountable problem faced by the collective church, over which we have no control. But each of us is a member of Christ's church (1 Corinthians 12:12–27), and as long as we individual members are sin-sick, so also is the body of Christ.

If we each assume others will catch the little foxes that are ruining our vineyard, the blossoms will all be eaten. We will never grow the fruit of maturity; our intimacy with the Bridegroom will never deepen. And the watching world will easily dismiss a bride so easily distracted by other, lesser loves.

I'll go first. As I consider this list of idols we often cherish in the church, I see several that have become not just good but ultimate things in my life. But there has been another idol in my life that God has recently revealed. It has been quietly gobbling blossoms in my relationship with him for years.

In chapter 1, I told you about my early memory of watching my father leave our family. The enemy's ploy was swift and sure: he lied to me about my lack of worth and told me I could protect myself from ever being rejected and abandoned again. He pointed out that I had been given many gifts that I could use to build an impregnable fortress around myself that no one could pull down or hurt me in. He offered me a life built on the foundation of self-effort and perfectionism.

Then he whispered this to my spirit: "And if a little glory splashes your way here and there, well, that will be our little secret."

As I agreed, self-idolatry set up shop in my life, and I unknowingly fed it for decades with a steady diet of achievement and approval. I basked in others' admiration, even depending on it to shore up my sense of worth. For years this unclean thing, this "little fox," sat in a dark closet in my spirit, quietly eating the blossoms in my relationship with God, stealing glory from him and sweet intimacy from us.

It took decades and a Spirit-directed conversation with a trusted friend to deliver me from the idols of performance, success, and approval—all rooted in the "little fox" of self-idolatry. But on the day the Holy Spirit put the searchlight on my heart (Psalm 139:23–24), he also gave me the ability to see and repent of self-idolatry. That very day I kicked that "little fox" out of my life! And it hasn't been back since.

This was hard and painful work, but it was from God. And it has birthed a deeper freedom in me than I've ever known. It has also fanned into flame my love for Jesus as never before.

Who but he would love me in spite of—and then love me out of—the ugliness that had stolen so much intimacy and fruitfulness from our relationship? When God delivered me from self-idolatry, I discovered that Jesus loves me with a fierceness I can barely fathom. He is jealous for my full devotion.

And, sister, he loves you in this passionate and patient way as well.

A Bride Without Spot or Blemish

As our love for Jesus reawakens, we will begin to trust that Jesus has fully paid our bride price. We will by faith put on the spotless bridal garments he provides. Clothed in his righteousness, we will resemble the One our hearts love. Then, and only then, will we stop hiding away from God—in fear, despair, shame, hopelessness, helplessness, disqualification, hunger, disappointment, isolation, and distraction—and hide instead in our Bridegroom's safe and loving arms. Sheltered there, we will receive all we need to arise as the radiant, triumphant bride he came to make us.

Then will the prophecy of Hosea 2:19–20 be fulfilled: "I will betroth you to me in righteousness and in justice, in steadfast love and in mercy. I will betroth you to me in faithfulness. And you shall know the LORD."

One day our Bridegroom will return and we will rejoice together in a magnificent wedding. In her book *Blessed*, Nancy Guthrie paints this glorious picture of what awaits us: "One day he is going to come again for us. He will arrive as a warrior king on a white horse to do away with everything that has brought us pain and sorrow. And then he will come to us as a bridegroom so that our eternal marriage can begin. We'll finally have the intimacy with him we've always longed for but have never been able to achieve or maintain. We will love him who first loved us."[8]

Enter the Sacred Refuge of Your Bridegroom

Sister, amid all the voices trying to capture your attention, Jesus—your first love—may be saying something like this to you:

> Beloved, you must know it. Your distractions grieve me. Your flirtations are killing our love. They are breaking my heart. I tell you now: catch for us these "little foxes" that seem so innocent but destroy the fruit in our vineyard.
>
> For my eyes and ears are upon my Father, waiting for his command to come back to the earth. When I return, I come for a bride who is wholly mine. Beloved, will your lamp be filled with oil? Will you be prepared for my return? Will you be ready for our wedding?
>
> I have gone to prepare a place for you with me in my Father's house. But there is much still to be done on the earth. So many of "the least of these" remain without help or hope— and who but my people can offer them both? So many of the lost have never heard my name. Who will reach them?
>
> For I will have a complete bride, from every tribe, tongue, and nation. You will only finish the task if your eyes are fixed upon me. Abide deeply in me, beloved bride, and you will receive all that you need.
>
> How I long for you. For you are my own dear body. Flesh of my flesh and bone of my bone. My blood runs in your veins and gives you life. When I came and took on flesh, I did so to betroth myself to you in love on the cross. Your bride price was high, but I paid it with all my heart for the joy set before me.
>
> I know that you long to return to our "first love" relationship. Nothing is holding you back from this. I have done all that is necessary to present you to myself as a radiant bride, without spot or wrinkle or any other blemish. When we are finally joined in marriage, you will have made yourself ready, clothed in fine linen, bright and pure. Perfect as I am perfect. Holy as

I am holy. And as you come forth, you will truly be a radiant bride, resplendent with the glory I have given you. And you shall lift your unveiled face before mine and behold my passion for you, my own beautiful, brave beloved.

On that day will my covenant vow be fulfilled: "I . . . take you to be my people, and I will be your God." Then, my sister, my bride, will I hear your dulcet voice say, "My Beloved is mine, and I am his."[9]

REST Under His Wings

Spend time quieting yourself in God's presence.

Release control.

1. In what ways have you struggled to believe in Jesus's love for you through life's crises?
2. In what ways—past or present—have you sensed yourself being wooed by Jesus? Sit before the Lord and spend some time simply worshiping him, releasing control of your life into his hands.

Father, I ask you to help me to come out of hiding and to enter fully into your sheltering love.

Exchange your *other lovers* for Jesus, your *beloved Bridegroom*.

3. Consider the ways that you have been hiding from God in distraction. What other lovers have stolen your affection for Jesus?
4. Write a prayer to the Lord, pouring out your heart to him. Let him know how you feel about this. Express your sorrow for "stepping out" on him.

Lord, I have missed you so much. I want to return to you. Jesus, I am basking in your mercy. Give me grace right now to rest deeply in your loving, sheltering arms. Please replace my distraction with the ability to fix my eyes on you. Replace my

escapism with your presence. Replace my fear with your love.
Help me, please, to love you with my whole heart, mind, soul,
and strength.

See yourself in union with Christ.

5. What are the "little foxes" in your life? How might God be revealing idolatry in your life and inviting you to repent and experience
   him in new and deeper ways?

6. What small change could help you live in light of your union with
   Christ? What could help you remember your first love?

Jesus, I entrust myself into your loving hands. With my eyes fixed
on you, I know you have made me part of your bride, without
spot or wrinkle. You are mine, and I am yours.

Trust Christ as the one who calls you beloved.

7. Create a breath prayer that you can use to recommit yourself to
   loving and trusting Jesus throughout your day. (For example:
   "Help me remember . . . my first love." "Awaken in me . . . more
   love for you." "Fewer distractions, Jesus . . . more of you.")

Afterword

DESPITE THE MANY issues that plague the church in the West, the church in the Southern and Eastern hemispheres is in large part thriving. Major church planting movements are even now springing up in Central and South America, across Asia, and throughout much of Africa. Jesus's bride will be a glorious tapestry of every color and ethnicity.

The apostle John described it this way: "After this I looked, and behold, a great multitude that no one could number, from every nation, from all tribes and peoples and languages [was] standing before the throne and before the Lamb" (Revelation 7:9).

If you are in Christ, sister, there will come a day when you and I will stand around the throne of Jesus Christ, the Lamb of God. When that day comes, if we look carefully, we might discern the faces of our sacred sisters from across time and space who in their crises found sacred refuge in Jesus.

There will be our sisters from Boston, beautiful and besotted with the Lover of their souls. Over there will be Eve, mother of the living, exultant to see the fulfillment of the Father's promise to send a Savior to undo the work of the serpent.

Our Midwest sisters will be there, standing shoulder-to-shoulder with their newest sisters, wooed through love.

Rhoda will be there, her heart's desire for safety and love finally fulfilled.

To our right will stand Rahab, chosen from the pagan city of Jericho to become an ancestor of the Savior.

Katrina will be there, reunited with her son, who reached home before she did.

In the distance I can see Deborah, Ruth, and the woman Jesus healed of bleeding.

Just over there are Mary and Martha, huddled with Lazarus, joy etched on their faces as they extol Jesus as the source of their resurrection and life.

And can you see her? Just a few rows ahead of us? It's Paige, the modern daughter of Deborah. Others of us will join her as "mothers in Israel" and beloved warriors of God. Having found sacred refuge, we will have obeyed God's call to shelter others.

There, too, will be multitudes of other women in our sacred sisterhood we have yet to meet. From every tribe, tongue, and people group, they are an integral part of Jesus's spotless bride. I will be there, as will you. And we will stand and worship with one voice: our mothers, sisters, aunts, fathers, brothers, husbands, and sons also gathered in worship of the Lamb.

Be encouraged, sister. This picture is not just a future hope. It can be our present reality. Our lives may still be subject to hardship, but our solace is Christ himself, our Promised Savior, Pursuer, Protector, Healer, Provider, Salvation, Redeemer, Resurrection and Life, Warrior, and breathtaking Bridegroom. How he longs for us, his bride, to experience the sacred refuge of his embrace!

On that day Jesus will fulfill his promise to restore all that has been broken in this fallen world, including the crises you have experienced. Our suffering will meet with pure solace when we are comforted by the Prince of Peace.

What John saw as a vision, we will experience:

> Then I saw a new heaven and a new earth, for the first heaven
> and the first earth had passed away, and the sea was no more.
> And I saw the holy city, new Jerusalem, coming down out of
> heaven from God, prepared as a bride adorned for her hus-

band. And I heard a loud voice from the throne saying, "Behold, the dwelling place of God is with man. He will dwell with them, and they will be his people, and God himself will be with them as their God. He will wipe away every tear from their eyes, and death shall be no more, neither shall there be mourning, nor crying, nor pain anymore, for the former things have passed away."

And he who was seated on the throne said, "Behold, I am making all things new" (Revelation 21:1–5).

How he longs for us, his bride, to experience the sacred refuge of his embrace!

Sister, though this vision gives such hope for our future, we won't become that "bride adorned for her husband" by settling for half-hearted devotion to Jesus. Thankfully, his great love and complete redemption have paved the way for us out of hiding in distraction with lesser lovers. The way into sacred refuge is open before us. How will we respond to the Lover of our souls?

Entering the Sacred Refuge of Jesus's Embrace

Let's consider one last story from the bride of Christ. As you hear her speak, may her experience become yours. If we could hear the bride, I imagine she'd describe her journey into the sacred refuge of Jesus's embrace like this:

> Still dressed in last night's finery and with shoes in hand, I am sneaking out in the early morning from a hotel room. I have just left the warm bed of my other lover, Comfort.
>
> Tiptoeing down the hall, desperately looking for the exit,

I notice the doors to other rooms. Each bears a name plate: Control, Security, Affluence, Approval, Success. Yes, I have been with them, as well.

Sorrow and shame overwhelm me. I feel dirty and unworthy to be called Jesus's bride. Overcome with feelings of guilt, I almost slide down the wall of the hallway, heartsick. But longing to escape this place of trysts and "making time" with these other lovers keeps me moving. There must be a way out of here!

A light shining at the end of the hallway catches my attention. Looking up, I see a form standing still and solitary. He looks straight at me.

I know at once it is Jesus.

He has been here, and he has seen it all. My spiritual adulteries have angered and saddened him, but he is here. Jesus has come for me.

His eyes are upon me.

He sees me. He knows me.

And yet he still loves me.

I feel my heart begin to quicken.

Mercy pours out of him in spite of what he knows.

What kind of Lover is this? He is untamed and like no other.

A momentous decision stands before me. I can either continue to entertain my other lovers, or I can part company with them forever and be fully his.

And in the moment I know this: Jesus's love is still for me, his blood has fully covered my adultery. Despite his broken heart, he has not given up on me.

I drop my baggage in the hallway. I won't be needing it anymore.

Fixing my eyes on Jesus, I begin to walk toward him. One moment, Jesus seems so far away. In another, he is near.

I am captivated by his eyes. Full of love, they compel me to take another step. And another.

I am moving more quickly now. Because all that is within me longs to be as near to him as possible. Nothing must part us again.

His eyes are upon me in love and desire. He wants me with him.

I am only dimly aware of the hotel hallway now. The plaques on the doors are fading from my sight.

The closer I get to Jesus, the more clearly I see him.

And now I perceive that he is not just surrounded by light. He *is* light. And life. And love.

He is the love of my life.

Everything within me is yearning to be with him. Nothing else will do.

As I approach Jesus, I am enveloped by his light.

And then this wonder dawns upon me: I am no longer in the hallway of a hotel.

I am now walking an aisle in a place of perfect peace and beauty and worship. The roof has given way to majestic trees. A kaleidoscope of flowers lines my path. Blossoming vines spread their sweet fragrance overhead. In the distance, I hear the soft call of a turtledove.

And still I walk, quickening my pace, toward my Savior, my Lover, my Lord.

The view is misty before me. Am I crying?

No, it is a veil, and I am wearing a robe of purest white, without spot or wrinkle. My Bridegroom's gift.

Just steps away from my Lover now, his eyes continue to draw me nearer.

Nearer.

Nearer.

I see his hand reach out for me and pull me to himself.

This is bliss. To see myself, now made beautiful, reflected in his luminous eyes. There is only love here.

No condemnation, no sadness, no heartbreak, no disappointment. Just his tender affection and fierce passion sheltering and surrounding me.

My Bridegroom grasps the edge of my veil and lifts it slowly over my head, revealing my upturned face before him. Our eyes are locked upon one another. There is no other.

My Beloved is mine, and I am his.

Next Steps

WELL DONE, SISTER! You've completed the initial leg of your journey to sacred refuge. Now it's time to take the next steps.

Get Connected

Although you may feel like you are all alone in your faith walk, you're not. God is raising up other women like you who are tired of hiding out in their own lives. We sense God is offering us more. He is empowering us to experience sacred refuge together in a sacred sisterhood. Here's how you can be part of that movement:

- Join the Brave Beloved Facebook group to connect with other women who are seeking to live and serve from a place of sacred refuge in Christ.
- Check out the Brave Beloved YouTube channel for further teaching to encourage your ongoing steps toward finding shelter in God.
- Share how you are experiencing God's sheltering love and presence by using #SacredRefuge when you post on Facebook, Instagram, or Pinterest.
- Consider reading *Sacred Refuge* with a small group of other women and using the study guide in appendix B to help you apply its truths. You can spur each other on to find, abide in, and share sacred refuge with others.
- Bring a Sacred Refuge retreat (in person or virtual) to your church. (Visit bravebeloved.com.)

Get a Free Resource

Perhaps you have taken your first few steps toward dwelling in the shelter of the Most High. Go to bravebeloved.com (or use this QR code) to access a free downloadable resource that will encourage you in that process. This guide to sacred refuge will give you practical steps toward experiencing Jesus as your Beloved and bravely responding to him with your whole heart.

Acknowledgments

DURING MY WORK to create *Sacred Refuge*, I have been surrounded—and sheltered—by a community of people who encouraged me as the book took shape. Though there are many others, I am especially indebted to the following:

Rob Rienstra, my first and best editor, who walked through this long process with patience and grace, serving me through many hours of discussion and prayer about the content of the book. Two are indeed better than one (Ecclesiastes 4:9)!

My mother, Beth Silvercloud, whose prayers and encouragement fueled my ability to write during a challenging season of life, and whose own journey out of hiding and into the shelter of God's love has inspired my own.

My children prayed and cheered me on in the writing process.

My friend Amy Lanclos brought her considerable editing skills to bear on the earliest drafts with intelligence, care, and precision. *Sacred Refuge* is a better book for her careful sifting of words and ideas—a labor of love for God, for the truth, and for me.

My friend Christy Frain saw the value of *Sacred Refuge* from its inception in March 2020 and prayed for it from then until its birth.

My friend Maggie Rowe carried this book in her heart and faithfully lifted me in prayer throughout the writing and editing process.

God used friend and writing mentor Donna Partow to help me get out of the way.

Friend Patricia Durgin from Marketers on a Mission asked me hard questions that gave the book clearer focus.

Other friends and spiritual midwives also supported me in prayer, forming a sacred sisterhood that carried me through: Doreen Clark, Christina Landry, Judy Childs, Cindy Woods, Kathy Owsley, and the muskoxen prayer circle; Kristin Watson, Alicia Manley, Andrea Cashdollar, Heather Kloth, Rebecca Burnett, Kelly Sites, Irene Cejka, Janet Newberry, Melinda Lysiak, Rachael Long, Kim Beckworth, Linda Lowder, Beth Caudill, Cathy Njoya, Megan Stephenson, Anne St. Clair, Ann Katherine Bryan and family, Sally Mulloy, Paula McKinney, Susie Kawa, Janinne Abel, Dana Little, Sherie Meyers, Ann Moore, Lynn Park, Kathy Whitworth, Teresa Robertson, and many others too numerous to mention. I am also grateful for David and Heather Hauser, Matt and Dara Lynn Rieger, and my entire church family who prayed me through both cancer and the writing of this book! Thanks also go to my work colleagues for their prayerful support, especially Dane Fowlkes and the Church Engagement team.

Deep gratitude for Susan Hunt, whose foundational work on spiritual mothering (found in her book of the same title) continues to bear fruit in my life.

I am deeply indebted to Rachel Kirsch, gifted developmental editor Amy Tol, and the team at Kregel for their insightful edits and beautiful design features that helped shape this book into its current form.

Cynthia Ruchti, my agent at Books & Such Literary Management, your Spirit-directed ability to navigate challenges and discern God's path helped make *Sacred Refuge* possible.

Appendix A

What Is Sacred Sisterhood?

I WAS GIVEN an extraordinary gift the year I turned eighteen—a full scholarship to a Seven Sisters women's college. With it came an education of the highest quality among a remarkable group of curious and gifted women. There is no denying the benefit of women investing in the lives of other women, and I am deeply grateful for the generosity of alumnae who made my journey possible. During my college experience, I learned to trust my voice raised in constructive debate, to listen well to others' ideas, and to enter a powerful network of alums who opened doors of opportunity for me. That was decades ago.

As beneficial as my secular connections were, I discovered a different, even better, kind of sisterhood during my college years. It happened in the context of relationships with other women on campus who were also seeking to follow Jesus. Though we came from very different backgrounds, and in some cases other countries, we had a deep and instant bond in our common love for Jesus Christ. Joined in him, we discovered the power of *sacred sisterhood*.

I have experienced this same phenomenon throughout my life, in my own culture and around the globe. It's a sacred sisterhood that connects me deeply with women who are walking in the same direction, hearts beating for the same cause, eyes fixed on the same goal: Jesus.

The Power of Sacred Sisterhood

So what makes sacred sisterhood work? God does. This sisterhood's power source is his love for women and his design of women as life-givers. As we live out this calling together and abide deeply in Jesus, he empowers us to rise up as truth-speakers, vision-casters, change-makers, and movement-leaders.

- We learn how to "spur one another on toward love and good deeds" (Hebrews 10:24 NIV).
- We fulfill our design as spiritual mothers who train younger women in how to love God and others (Titus 2:2–5).
- We serve as spiritual midwives of the good and godly purposes God is giving birth to in our sisters' lives (Galatians 4:19).

When a group of women pursue these ends from the same center (a relationship with Jesus Christ) and toward the same end (God's glory), a sacred sisterhood is born. Fueled by a growing sense of our identity as God's beloved, we call forth faith-based bravery in each other. This is a courage rooted in deep dependence on God to show up and repair this broken world through us, his daughters.

We leave behind personal agendas and self-aggrandizement for a life laid down for others. When each woman in a sacred sisterhood circle fixes her eyes on Jesus and helps her sisters move together in his purposes, we watch God's life-giving power unleashed. And no power of hell will stop it (Matthew 16:18).

The Community of Sacred Sisterhood

A few months ago, I spent a week at the ocean. Picture a sugar-sand beach and clear aqua waters. Sunny days in the midseventies and nights in the fifties.

One dusky evening as I was packing up to return to the condo, I noticed a group of women making their way back to the beach from a nearby cottage. Eight to ten of them carried food, tiki lamps, and beach chairs toward the water. They arranged beach chairs in a circle around a cheerful fire. Someone played a guitar and they started worshiping. This was a gathering I wanted to join!

As the temperature dropped, several of the women pulled out blankets, wrapping them around themselves and then extending the blankets over their sisters' backs to ward off the chill. It seemed there was always room for one more under those commodious and comforting covers.

This is the kind of sisterhood that Jesus longs for us to enjoy. He has made it all possible. He is in the middle of this sacred sisterhood, the source of our life-giving capacity, our healing, and our growth. As we abide in him, he fills us with abundant life, deepening love, Spirit-directed power, and clear vision.

We begin by learning how to live in—and from—his sacred refuge. That's the message of this book. Then God empowers us to extend the blanket over others, to share with them the shelter we've found. That's when life as we've known it begins to change. That's when God begins to change the world *through* us.

The Center of Sacred Sisterhood

I recently saw a sweatshirt that proclaimed, "As strong as the woman next to me." In a secular sisterhood, this dynamic might truly read "*only* as strong as the woman next to me." Without a source of strength outside herself, each woman only has limited power based on her own resources. In time, they will fall short.

In a sacred sisterhood, however, "as strong as the woman next to me" becomes wonderfully true as each woman, a temple of the Holy Spirit (1 Corinthians 6:19), taps into God's inexhaustible resources to share with others: wisdom (Ephesians 1:17), truth (John 14:25–26), encouragement (Romans 15:5), comfort (2 Corinthians 1:3–4), and guidance (Acts 16:6–10).

Notice that all of this comes from the Spirit of Christ. He is the center that holds sacred sisters together, despite differences in age, personality, interests, and culture. We share sacred shelter with one another through the gifts the Holy Spirit gives (1 Corinthians 12:4–11). When we gather as sisters to study God's Word or pray or connect, we are actually gathering in his presence. We are inviting Jesus Christ to sit in the center of our circle and direct by his Spirit all that is said and done. We acknowledge that he is our source and that fulfilling his will is the goal of our sisterhood.

The Refuge of Sacred Sisterhood

Perhaps you will want to gather a group of other women to work though the truths in *Sacred Refuge*. Scripture makes it clear: "Two are better than one" (Ecclesiastes 4:9). It may help you to make the journey out of hiding and into a permanent change of address in God's sacred refuge if you go together.

In the final chapters, you may have begun to sense that God wants to use your sacred sisterhood as a nursery for exponential personal and spiritual growth. What if your circle of friends became a group of spiritual midwives who help each other birth the new life direction God has prepared you all to walk in and the new ministries God has prepared for you to lead? What if God called you to help one another catalyze change in your communities as his brave beloved ones—waging war against the brokenness and isolation all around us with the presence and power of Christ?

How the world needs women who live and love from a place of sacred refuge! How much further might our ministry reach if our sacred sisters have our backs and pray us through?

To that end, here is my prayer for you:

> *Father, you know for what purposes you are calling your daughters into sacred sisterhood at this hour. How the world needs their life-giving design, their tender hearts, their powerful relational skills, and their fierce desire to protect and nurture others.*

Would you help your daughters to invite Jesus to be the source and the power supply of their time together? Would you send your Holy Spirit to guide their discussions, thoughts, and prayers? Would you help each woman begin to live in—and from—sacred refuge?

And having been sheltered there, may she seek you about how to shelter others in these darkening days. Be at work for your daughters' good, the world's healing, and your glory! We ask all this in Jesus's mighty name. Amen.

Appendix B

Study Guide

PERHAPS YOU ARE reading *Sacred Refuge* on your own. Or maybe you have gathered a friend or two (or eight) to walk through its truths together.

If it's your intention that your Bible study circle become a sacred sisterhood, then commit yourselves and your group to God. Invite the Lord Jesus to dwell in your midst and to help you fix your eyes on him. Ask him to fill you with his Holy Spirit—that he may be the source of the wisdom, compassion, comfort, and love you share with one another.

The reality of living in a world infected by sin and the consequences of the fall means we come to this circle of sisters with broken stories and hurting hearts. In that context we might suffer together, bearing one another's burdens. But in light of the gospel, we can also share solace (holy comfort) with one another. Pursue this as a goal of your time together.

As you encourage each other to enter God's sacred refuge, create a safe place to talk honestly about the ways you may be hiding from God (or even each other). Commit to keeping one another's confidences. Agree that what is shared in the circle stays in the circle—unless the issue needs deeper care from a seasoned counselor.

Begin each time together in prayer, asking the Holy Spirit who inspired the words of Scripture to also come and illuminate them as you open God's Word together.

And then finish your time together in prayer, ministering to your sisters by God's power.

Chapter 1: Loved
Finding Shelter in the Promised Savior

Consider the following as you discern what God is saying to you through the story of our sister Eve. May he guide your steps out of hiding and into his sacred refuge.

1. How are you currently wrestling with this chapter's key question, "Can God restore what's been broken?"
2. What crisis are you facing right now? What about it is most daunting to you?
3. How do you trace your struggle's roots to the fall—and the destruction the enemy has wreaked in our lives ever since?
4. Like Eve, have you ever thought you had to *do* something, so you could *have* something, so you could *be* someone? Where has this led you?
5. When Adam and Eve realized they had broken fellowship with God, they hid from him. Have you also been hiding from God? What form has this taken?
6. Just as God pursued Eve, he is pursuing you. How do you see evidence of that?
7. What does God's extraordinary promise of a Savior who will crush the serpent (and his work) mean to you right now?
8. How does the sacred refuge God provided for Adam and Eve resemble the kind of shelter you need?
9. The promise of a Savior gave Eve tremendous hope. What feelings surface for you when you consider that the refuge God built for Eve is the very place he's inviting you into?
10. Do you believe that there is a safe place in Christ where you are truly seen, deeply known, and unconditionally loved? Instead of

questioning God's Word as Eve did, how might trusting God's
Word bring you true shelter in your current storm?

If you have never trusted in the Promised Savior, Jesus Christ,
before, perhaps God is calling you into a relationship with himself
through the power of his Holy Spirit. Will you respond? If so, this
prayer may serve as a guide:

Prayer for Entering Sacred Refuge for the First Time

*Father, the crisis I am dealing with has caused me to wonder if
you are real or good. It has put me in hiding. But now I sense a
stirring in my spirit. I trust that you are at work—maybe even
through my suffering—to call me out of hiding and into a forever
relationship with you.*

*I want to come home to you. I admit that my life falls short of
your holiness, and I ask for your forgiveness. I believe that Jesus
Christ went to the cross and died on my behalf to remove my sin,
give me his righteousness, and restore my relationship with you.
I now commit my life to you; I put all of myself into your hands.*

*I trust that your love for me is great, Father. Please fill me
with your Holy Spirit. Having received Jesus, now help me to
continue resting in him. I ask this in Jesus's name. Amen.*

Chapter 2: Known
Finding Shelter in the One Who Sees You

Consider the following as you discern what God is saying to you
through the story of Hagar. May he guide your steps out of hiding
and into his sacred refuge.

1. Share about a time you ran away or hit a dead end.
2. How are you working through this chapter's key question, "Can
   God make a way forward from here?"

3. How do you relate to Hagar's story?
4. Have you been running from an unfair situation? Has your own pride caused you (or others) to suffer?
5. How have you dealt with these situations? Have you been running from God?
6. What does it mean to you that God is "the One who sees me"? If Jesus asked you these questions right now, how would you respond?

   Where have you been?
   Where are you going?
7. How has God *pursued* you? How have you responded to God's pursuit of you?
8. How has God *protected* you? Have you thanked him for his care?
9. What has God *promised* you? Have you ever lost hope that God will keep his promises to you?
10. What is a step you could take to come out of hiding and turn toward the Lord who sees, knows, and loves you?
11. If Jesus asked you the following questions, which one would most spark your attention and why? How would you respond?

Beloved, will you now exchange years of regret for an eternity of joyful anticipation?

Beloved, will you now exchange hiding in hopelessness for a growing experience of my delight in you?

Beloved, will you now exchange numbing self-hatred for your inheritance—forever—of my love?

End your time by praying for one another, asking God to make a clear path forward for each of you in your current crisis.

Chapter 3: Forgiven
Finding Shelter in Christ's Righteousness

Consider the following as you discern what God is saying to you through the story of our sister caught in adultery. May he guide your steps out of hiding and into his sacred refuge.

1. Share about a time you messed up as a child—and hid.
2. How are you wrestling right now with this chapter's key question, "Can God free me from the shame of my sin?"
3. How can you relate to the story of the woman caught in adultery? Have you ever experienced having your sin publicly revealed?
4. What shape does shame tend to take in your life? (Do you try to hide certain things from God or others? Or struggle with negative, shameful thoughts? Or try to compensate with good works?)
5. How did Jesus level the playing field in this story?
6. How is Jesus able to offer the woman freedom from condemnation?
7. Jesus asked the woman, "Where are they? Has no one condemned you?" If Jesus has removed your condemnation, how can you now respond to the enemy's accusations from here on?
8. How does Jesus's treatment of this woman encourage you in your current crisis?
9. What do you love most about how Jesus created sacred refuge for this woman? How does this reflect your own deepest desires?

Pray for one another to come out of hiding in long-held shame and enter the freedom Jesus purchased for you.

Chapter 4: Healed
Finding Shelter in the Great Physician

Consider the following as you discern what God is saying to you through the story of our sister with chronic bleeding. May he guide your steps out of hiding and into his sacred refuge.

1. Share about a time you or a loved one experienced serious illness.

2. How are you currently working through this chapter's key question, "Can God restore my health and peace?"

3. How can you relate to the story of the woman with an issue of blood? Are you facing illness right now? Is it physical, emotional, or spiritual?

4. Has a health crisis ever caused you to hide from God, assuming that sickness was punishment from him or the result of your sin?

5. Like the woman in Luke 8, have you ever fallen into hopelessness (or are you there right now)?

6. What lie (about God or yourself) has caused you to look for shelter outside of the true shelter of Jesus?

7. What if the deepest desire of your heart turned out to be exactly what God most wants to give you? Is this something you believe? Why or why not?

8. How did Jesus *see* the woman? How did Jesus *know* her? How did he *love* her?

9. Do you believe that Jesus likewise *sees* you, *knows* you, and *loves* you?

10. In what part of your life do you most long to experience the *shalom* (deep peace) and wholeness that Jesus restored to the woman? Share one prayer request with the group that expresses where you'd most like to experience healing and peace.

As you end this study time, take turns praying for one another to be healed and made whole in Jesus.

Chapter 5: Provided For
Finding Shelter in the God of All Supply

Consider the following as you discern what God is saying to you through the story of the widow and the oil. May he guide your steps out of hiding and into his sacred refuge.

1. Share about a time you had an unmet need. How did you handle that crisis?
2. How are you connecting with this chapter's key question, "Can I really trust God to meet my needs?"
3. In what way does the widow's plight mirror your own? Are you in significant debt with no help in sight?
4. Are there any financial situations that have put you into hiding? Or in what ways have you hidden your true identity behind money and the things it can buy?
5. When the widow knew her debts were far more than she could pay, she could have gone into hiding—in denial or other destructive directions. But she didn't. How does her example instruct you?
6. What is the status of your "spiritual debt"? Have you fully entrusted that debt into Jesus's hands? Why or why not?
7. Read Genesis 22:1–14. What aspect of God's character is on display in this story?
8. How has God revealed himself to you as Jehovah Jireh, your Provider, in the past?
9. God is a lavish Provider. The widow received an abundant supply because she trusted God's unlikely plan: "Borrow vessels from all your neighbors, empty vessels and not too few" (2 Kings 4:3). What might it look like for you to take a step of faith like this in your own life? (Or how might you be limiting the flow of God's blessing because you *haven't* taken steps of faith?)
10. In what area of your life do you most need to experience God as your faithful Provider?
11. What are some practices that could help you build trust in the sacred refuge of God's faithful provision?

End your time by praying for one another's needs, trusting God to provide all that is needed.

Chapter 6: Rescued
Finding Shelter in Christ's Mercy

Consider the following as you discern what God is saying to you through the story of our sister Rahab. May he guide your steps out of hiding and into his sacred refuge.

1. When did you most need a fresh start in life?
2. How do you resonate with this chapter's key question, "Can God give someone with my past a new beginning?"
3. What part of Rahab's story do you most connect with? Why?
4. How did God pursue Rahab? What promise did he make to her through the spies? How did he protect her?
5. How has God sheltered you, as he did Rahab, from judgment?
6. Read 1 John 2:1–2: "But if anyone does sin, we have an advocate with the Father, Jesus Christ the righteous. He is the propitiation for our sins, and not for ours only but also for the sins of the whole world." What does it mean to you that Jesus is your propitiation?
7. How has Jesus sheltered you under his mercy? In his grace?
8. Until God gave her faith, Rahab may have put her trust in her ability to work hard enough to provide her own shelter. The citizens of Jericho trusted in their city's massive walls to protect them. What walls or other false constructs have you trusted in, other than Christ?
9. Like Rahab, do you sometimes feel like an outsider? How has God "invited you in"?
10. Have you felt disqualified from ministering to others—like God could never use someone with your past? How is God speaking to you through Rahab? Through Catherine?
11. How is God using Rahab's story to give you hope that he is also rewriting your story?

Pray for one another, asking God to give you sacred refuge and a new beginning.

Chapter 7: Redeemed
Finding Shelter in Your Kinsman-Redeemer

Consider the following as you discern what God is saying to you through the story of our sister Naomi. May he guide your steps out of hiding and into his sacred refuge.

1. Share about a time you knowingly walked away from God.
2. Have you ever asked this chapter's key question: "Can I still come home, even when I've wandered from God?"
3. What is your Moab? Where has the grass seemed greener and captured your attention away from God or others? Or has a crisis outside your control caused you to flee?
4. In what ways can you relate to Naomi's deep sense of discontent? Bitterness?
5. Is God using your crisis to offer you unexpected shelter? How?
6. Have you been separated from God's people? What effect has that had on your life?
7. How might God be using your discontent or losses to draw you closer to himself and his people?
8. How does the story of Boaz covering Ruth and Naomi as their kinsman-redeemer touch you?
9. What aspects of Jesus as your Kinsman-Redeemer mean the most to you? Do you find it easy or difficult to let him shelter you? Why?
10. Where do you need to experience the fullness Jesus alone can give you?
11. What is Jesus saying to you through this story? What do you want to say in response to him?

End your study by praying for each other. Ask God to help you trust your losses to him and find fullness in both his redeeming love and the community of his people.

Chapter 8: Comforted
Finding Shelter in Christ's Compassion

Consider the following as you discern what God is saying to you through the story of our sister Mary of Bethany. May he guide your steps out of hiding and into his sacred refuge.

1. Share about a significant loss you have endured.
2. How can you relate to this chapter's key question, "When my heart is broken in disappointment, can I still trust God?"
3. Where do you find yourself in the story of John 11:1–44? What situation in your life parallels that of Mary and Martha?
4. Do you most relate to Martha or Mary? Why?
5. Have you ever asked God to come and change everything, and he seemed to be saying, "Not yet"? How did that experience affect your relationship with Jesus?
6. About what situation have you been saying, "If only . . ." (If only God would . . . If only God had . . . If only I had . . .)? Where has this taken you?
7. Have you been hiding from God and heartbreak? In deep disappointment? What lies, if any, have you begun to believe about God? Yourself? The future?
8. If someone told you, "The master is here, and he is asking for you," how would you respond?
9. In John 11 Jesus asked, "Where have you laid him?" He might ask you today, "What is it that has died in your life?" Is it a person that you thought you could never live without? Is it a dream that you once longed for and worked toward, but now appears to be dead? Is it hope for your children and grandchildren? What is it that feels dead in your life right now? Will you trust Jesus to bring life out of that death in your life?
10. What stone/barrier has kept you from experiencing resurrection life in union with Christ?

11. After he raised Lazarus from the dead, Jesus commanded that they "remove the graveclothes." Even after Jesus resurrects us and brings life out of our death scenarios, there may be unholy habits that still bind us up. What is standing between you and total freedom? Will you confess and release it now to the Lord?

Pray for one another. Ask God to "roll away the stone" and "remove the graveclothes" in your loss—that he may bring life out of death for you.

Chapter 9: Empowered
Finding Shelter in Our Divine Warrior

Consider the following as you discern what God is saying to you through the story of our sister Deborah. May he guide your steps out of hiding and into his sacred refuge.

1. Share about a fight that came to your doorstep.
2. How do you process this chapter's key question, "Can God empower me to fight for others and offer them the sacred refuge he has given me?"
3. What kinds of battles are you facing right now? Are they personal or on a bigger scale?
4. Where do you see truth being attacked in our culture today? What concerns does this raise for you?
5. How do the battles of our day resemble that of Deborah's time?
6. How is "village life" ceasing in our culture?
7. What aspects of Deborah's role as a "mother in Israel" are most compelling to you?
8. Of the many possible definitions for *qûm* ("arise"), which one(s) is the Holy Spirit highlighting for you? (See p. 192.)
9. What would it look like in your life to exchange your own "power" for God's might?

10. Deborah got right in the middle of the action and had a front-row seat to a miraculous work of God. What about you? Have there been times when you were like the tribes who didn't answer the call and missed out on receiving blessing—and blessing others? Have there been times when, like our sister Deborah, you arose and joined the battle?

11. As you increasingly experience the shelter of God in your own life, how might God be calling you to arise and shelter others?

End your session by praying about how you think God may be calling you to offer others the sacred refuge he has given you. Lift all this to God in prayer, asking for his guidance and provision.

Chapter 10: Beloved
Finding Shelter in the Arms of the Bridegroom

Consider the following as you discern what God is saying to you through Song of Solomon 2, an allegory of the love between the Bridegroom (Jesus) and the bride of Christ (the church). May he guide your steps out of hiding and into his sacred refuge.

1. As part of the body of Christ, how do you resonate with this chapter's key question, "Can Jesus awaken his bride, the church, and restore our first love for him?"

2. Are you surprised by the statistics related to the current "dechurching" movement? How have you seen evidence of this in your own family, church, or community?

3. What most concerns you about this trend—for yourself, your family and descendants, your church, your community, our nation, and the world?

4. Have you thought about yourself as part of the bride of Christ? Is the concept of God's passionate love for his bride new to you?

5. Reread Song of Solomon 2:8–16. Do you hear the Bridegroom's

longing for his bride? Do you hear Jesus's longing for you in these words?

6. How do you think this can be a "new season" of faithfulness for the church? How is the Lord calling us to "arise"? What part might he be calling you to play in this?

7. In verse 14, the Bridegroom calls his beloved out of hiding. What do the "clefts of the rock" and "crannies of the cliff" look like in your life? In what ways do you find yourself hiding from God?

8. In verse 15, the Bridegroom commands the beloved to "catch the foxes for us" that steal our fruit. What are the "little foxes" in your life? What is stealing your attention from Jesus?

9. What are some practical ways you can work at minimizing these distractions in your life—or new practices that might help you return to Jesus as your "first love"?

10. As part of the bride, how can you help your church community fix their eyes on Jesus, the Bridegroom? How might you work with other sisters to "walk the aisle" toward deeper union with him and obedience to him in these last days?

End your final session by praying for one another, asking God to help you arise as the brave, beloved bride of Christ in your own spheres of influence.

Sacred Refuge Prayer

FATHER, MY DAYS of hiding are over. Carry me, step-by-step, out of the place of fear and isolation I have mistaken for my permanent abode. Even in my current crisis, I turn away from darkness and despair. I lift my face into the light of your love. How I long to dwell in your presence and experience the precious refuge Jesus came to give me in himself. By faith, Lord, I nestle deeply under the refuge of your wings. By your grace and power, I ask you to:

- Call me out of fear, and grow in me a faith that rests deeply in the love of Jesus, my promised Savior.
- Call me out of despair as the One who sees me.
- Call me out of shame, and help me to experience you as my Protector.
- Call me out of hopelessness, and, as my Healer, fill me with your wholeness and peace.
- Call me out of helplessness, and allow me to experience you as my faithful Provider.
- Call me out of believing I am disqualified from serving you, and use my life to reveal you as the God who saves.
- Call me out of hunger and want, and as my Kinsman-Redeemer, fill me with your fullness.

- Call me in the midst of heartbreak to trust you as my Resurrection and Life.
- Call me out of isolation, and empower me to arise and follow you, my Divine Warrior, into battle.
- Call me away from distraction with other lovers, and help me fix my eyes on you, Jesus, my beloved Bridegroom.

Apart from you, I can do nothing. So I lean into your faithful, covenant-keeping love. And having found my safe place—now and forever—in you, help me to share your sacred refuge with others.

I ask this in the strong name of Jesus Christ. Amen.

Notes

Introduction

1. *Collins Dictionary*, s.v. "sacred," accessed May 6, 2024, www.col linsdictionary.com/dictionary/english/sacred.
2. *Collins Dictionary*, s.v. "refuge," accessed May 6, 2024, www.col linsdictionary.com/dictionary/english/refuge.
3. See Deuteronomy 4:41–43; Numbers 35:11–24; Joshua 20:1–9.

Chapter 1: Loved

1. Leif Hetland, *Called to Reign: Living and Loving from a Place of Rest* (Atlanta: Convergence Press, 2017), 60.
2. *The Westminster Standards: Confession of Faith, Larger Catechism, Shorter Catechism* (Suwanee, GA: Great Commission Publications, 2021), 80.
3. *The Works of Jonathan Edwards: Volume I–IV*, ed. Anthony Uhl (Ingersoll, ON: Devoted Publishing, 2019), 354.
4. Timothy Keller, *Walking with God Through Pain and Suffering* (New York: Penguin Random House, 2013), 6.
5. 1 John 4:18; Isaiah 53:3; John 14:12; Romans 5:2; Psalm 56:8; Song of Solomon 2:10.

Chapter 2: Known

1. Dane Ortlund, *Gentle and Lowly: The Heart of Christ for Sinners and Sufferers* (Wheaton, IL: Crossway, 2020), 99.
2. Genesis 16:1–15; Matthew 7:24–27; Matthew 28:20; Hebrews 13:5; 2 Corinthians 5:21; Luke 15:11–32; Revelation 21:5; 2 Corinthians 6:14; Isaiah 54:17; John 19:30.

Chapter 3: Forgiven

1. Timothy Keller, "The Humility of Jesus" (sermon), Redeemer Presbyterian Church, New York, NY, May 24, 1998.
2. Psalm 103:12; 2 Corinthians 10:5; 2 Corinthians 5:21; Song of Solomon 2:14; 1 John 1:8–9; Song of Solomon 2:6.

Chapter 4: Healed

1. Emily Brooks, "Waiting for Your Ticket: The Courage of Corrie ten Boom," *Emily Brooks* (blog), July 24, 2022, https://emily brookswriter.com/2022/07/24/waiting-for-your-ticket-the-cour age-of-corrie-ten-boom.
2. "Healing in His Wings," Got Questions, accessed August 15, 2023, https://www.gotquestions.org/healing-in-His-wings.html.
3. "Key Statistics for Breast Cancer," American Cancer Society, accessed July 3, 2023, https://www.cancer.org/cancer/types/breast -cancer/about/how-common-is-breast-cancer.html.
4. C. S. Lewis, *The Last Battle* (New York: Harper Trophy, 1984), 203.
5. Philippians 4:6–7; Colossians 3:3; Romans 8:28–29; John 13:23; Ephesians 3:16; Isaiah 53:5; Luke 8:44; Malachi 4:2; Psalm 91:4.

Chapter 5: Provided For

1. "Average American Debt," Ramsey Solutions, last updated May 13, 2024, www.ramseysolutions.com/debt/average-american-debt.
2. Ray Dillard, *Faith in the Face of Apostasy* (Phillipsburg, NJ: P&R Publishing, 1999), 95.
3. Robert Lowry, "Nothing But the Blood," 1876, public domain.
4. Galatians 4:4; 2 Corinthians 5:21; Hebrews 10:4–10; Romans 8:1; Luke 6:38; Ephesians 1:3; Isaiah 40:28–30; 1 John 1:9; Revelation 3:17–19.

Chapter 6: Rescued

1. Ray Vander Laan, "Fertility Cults of Canaan," That The World

May Know, accessed July 20, 2023, www.thattheworldmayknow .com/fertility-cults-of-canaan.

2. *Collins Dictionary*, s.v. "propitiate," accessed May 6, 2024, www .collinsdictionary.com/dictionary/english/propitiate.

3. Micah 7:19; Revelation 12:10; Ephesians 2:20–22; Philippians 3:13–14; Psalm 91:4.

Chapter 7: Redeemed

1. See Genesis 48:16; Exodus 6:6; Leviticus 27:9–25.

2. Andrew E. Hill and John H. Walton, *A Survey of the Old Testament* (Grand Rapids: Zondervan, 2009), 252.

3. "One in Three Practicing Christians Has Stopped Attending Church During COVID-19," Barna, July 8, 2020, www.barna .com/research/new-sunday-morning-part-2.

4. Iain Duguid, *Esther and Ruth*, Reformed Expository Commentary (Phillipsburg, NJ: P&R Publishing, 2005), 166.

5. See Isaiah 54:5; Hosea 2:16; Ezekiel 16:8–14.

6. Ruth 1:1; Luke 15; Revelation 3:17; Ezekiel 16:8; Colossians 2:8–10.

Chapter 8: Comforted

1. Journal entry used with permission.

2. Dane Ortlund, *Gentle and Lowly* (Wheaton, IL: Crossway, 2020), 26.

3. William Hendriksen, *John*, New Testament Commentary (Grand Rapids: Baker Books, 1983), 150.

4. Hendriksen, *John*, 150, italics in original.

5. Personal correspondence with the author. Used with permission.

6. John 11:25; John 10:10; 2 Corinthians 4:17–18; Revelation 7:17; John 11:43; Zephaniah 3:17.

Chapter 9: Empowered

1. Susan Hunt, *Spiritual Mothering: The Titus 2 Model for Women Mentoring Women* (Wheaton, IL: Crossway, 1992), 12.

2. Strong's Hebrew Lexicon (ESV), s.v. H6965 "qûm," Blue Letter Bible, accessed September 3, 2023, www.blueletterbible.org/lexi con/h6965/esv/wlc/0-1.

3. Dee Jepsen, *Women: Beyond Equal Rights* (Waco, TX: Word, 1984), 227.

4. John 10:10; Psalm 84:7; Romans 8:37; Romans 13:14; Ephesians 6:11–17; Hebrews 4:12; John 8:44; Matthew 16:17–29.

Chapter 10: Beloved

1. "The Great Dechurching," Missio Nexus, last updated August 21, 2023, www.missionexus.org/event/the-great-dechurching.

2. "One in Three Practicing Christians Has Stopped Attending Church During COVID-19," Barna, last updated July 8, 2020, www.barna.com/research/new-sunday-morning-part-2.

3. "Church Refugees," Dechurched.net, accessed October 2, 2023, www.dechurched.net/2015/12/22/church-refugees.

4. Iain M. Duguid, *Song of Songs*, Reformed Expository Commentary (Phillipsburg, NJ: P&R Publishing, 2016), 50.

5. Strong's Hebrew Lexicon (ESV), s.v. H6965 "qûm," Blue Letter Bible, accessed September 3, 2023, www.blueletterbible.org/lexi con/h6965/esv/wlc/0-1.

6. F. Landy, *Paradoxes of Paradise: Identity and Difference in the Song of Songs* (Sheffield: Almond, 1983), 240, quoted in Tremper Longman III, *Song of Songs*, New International Commentary on the Old Testament (Grand Rapids: Eerdmans, 2001), 124.

7. Marissa Postell Sullivan, "Pastors Identify Modern-day Idols, Comfort Tops List," Lifeway, last updated August 9, 2022, https://research.lifeway.com/2022/08/09/pastors-identify-modern-day-idols-comfort-tops-list.

8. Nancy Guthrie, *Blessed: Experiencing the Promise of the Book of Revelation* (Wheaton, IL: Crossway, 2022), 226.

9. Song of Solomon 2:14; Matthew 25:10; Matthew 25:40; Revelation 7:9; Hebrews 12:2; Genesis 2:23; Revelation 2:4; John 14:3; Revelation 19:7; Exodus 6:7; Song of Solomon 2:16; 2 Corinthians 3:18.

About the Author

LYNNE RIENSTRA is a recovering Pharisee and spiritual orphan—the result of growing up with three dads by the time she was nineteen (and of her own wayward heart). Through her mentoring, speaking, and writing, she leads women out of hiding and into a transforming encounter with the living God. In that place, they discover their identities as his brave beloved, rising up to restore our broken world as carriers of God's love and presence.

Lynne has followed a series of callings: English teacher, corporate insurance broker, pastor's wife, women's ministry leader, homeschooling mom, and development professional. Since 2013, she has served as a regional director for Samaritan's Purse. She has traveled to twenty-six countries on five continents (including Uganda, Liberia, Peru, Ecuador, Slovakia, North Korea, Iraq, Singapore, and Kenya, where she lived for a summer among the Maasai).

Whether leading a group of women in Bible study, leading a group of ministry partners to see God at work around the globe, or leading a group of women on a weekend retreat (she's taught thousands of women across the country over the last twenty-five years), Lynne revels in guiding others in the ultimate adventure: experiencing God's lavish love for them.

Lynne has contributed to *Decision*, *Georgia Life*, and to the books *Leading Ladies: Discover Your God-Grown Strategy for Success* (Bold

Vision Books), *Long Wandering Prayer* (IVP), and *Rekindle the Flame* (Bethany House). Her work has also appeared in *Arise Daily* online devotionals.

She holds a BA in English from Smith College and a Certificate in Spiritual Formation from the Transforming Center in Wheaton, Illinois. Lynne is a member of the AWSA (Advanced Writers and Speakers Association).

Serving alongside her husband, Rob, a senior pastor, gives Lynne much joy, as do their two adult children and granddaughters. She loves Earl Grey tea, all things French, period dramas, reading C. S. Lewis and Elizabeth Goudge, and scoring vintage clothing finds.

You can book Lynne for your event, or as a podcast or TV guest, at lynnerienstra.com and bravebeloved.com. Listen to her *Brave Beloved* podcast and access her teaching on YouTube. Lynne can also be found on Facebook, Pinterest, Instagram, and X.